To
B Bless

THE EMPOWERED *Life*

4/5/16 -
To my Beloved
Daughter Missie

From
Mother

JERRY M. CARTER, JR.

DEDICATION

This book is dedicated to my family for being a source of inspiration and strength. And, to Calvary Church for helping me live the Empowered Life!

The Empowered Life
by Jerry M. Carter, Jr.

For information, address:

The Church Online, LLC
1500 Ardmore Blvd.
Suite 402
Pittsburgh, PA 15221

International Standard Book Number: 978-1-940786-27-8

Library of Congress Catalogue Card Number: Available Upon Request

Printed in the United States of America

First Edition, May, 2015

Trademarks

TABLE OF CONTENTS

1

A CHURCH GOD TRUSTS

LEARNING TO LOVE & TRUST FOR A MORE SATISFIED & FULFILLED LIFE

TRUST AND TRYING SOMETHING NEW

Trust is an interesting concept. We often inherently trust our family members due to a long history of living with them and loving them through the good and the bad. We sometimes do not trust others—co-workers, new acquaintances, and community members that we see every day in the local diner, the post office, or the grocery store. It is, in fact, human to be mistrustful. In this world of identity theft and countries and religions at odds with one another, it is prudent to be cautious. Do we readily reach out to others? Do we include in our family those who are in need or maybe looking for friendship or companionship? Do we add to our lives people and experiences that will enrich us or move us in some way? Or—do we stay too cautious? Too guarded? God often needs us to be open, trustful and loving. He needs us to reach out and to share ourselves and our faith—our experiences and love with others. Are we up to the task? And, why does it seem so difficult, at times, to do just that? Test ourselves. Become a mover—a believer—someone who shapes others and the world around us.

Trust is an interesting concept.

At times, in our busy lives, we see trying to trust others as components to a happy life—expanded fellowship, new friends, work delegated to others, feelings shared and stresses alleviated. Other times, it is not so easy. Many times, we find ourselves in life, wondering why we are feeling left out. Either we are new at work or we've joined a new church—maybe we've even moved to a new neighborhood or started school. From the outside, it often seems like we don't fit or being the new person is something that is never going to be part of our persona. Looking to expand ourselves professionally or academically or to better our situations in life or in church fellowship seems daunting in that things that are new can also be unfriendly or appear uncomfortable at first. Sometimes, in a nutshell, it is hard to see how God wants to add you to his flock—to a particular church—or to a particular task in life.

OUR SCRIPTURE REFERENCE

In Acts 2:47b, the verse clearly reads "...and the Lord added to the church daily those such as should be saved..." In another version, it clearly says, "and the Lord added to their number daily those who were being saved...." "Further, the Lord added..." It doesn't say people simply joined a church; it says "and the Lord added..." On top of that, the verb "added" is in the imperfect tense, which means that the Lord "kept adding." He never stopped and has made it so that it will never stop! There is something profound in these simple lines—this concept of adding and allowing others into a life—into a ministry or a church. It is important to note here, that, as much as it appears that church growth is and was a mere human activity, it was not; it IS not. Today and back in the day of Jesus, folks weren't just church shopping; they were being added, trusted, by the Lord. And, in this concept—this adding people—trusting them to live and love in the church—the question arises: Can you simply leave the church if the Lord has added you to it? You can't get mad and walk away, because you didn't just join. A run-in with someone in the choir couldn't run you away.

It's hard to justify leaving when you become upset, especially when the Lord has added you. Is this significant? And, further, how is it significant? Is it one thing to be trusted by the Lord so that he adds you to his church? Is it another to let this be a life lesson for all who are struggling with how to fit in the church—and how to make others fit into our lives? Keep in mind, staying in the Lord's church as chosen members was probably expected. I mean, it wasn't because these people liked the way the building looked —because…. as a matter of fact, this early group of believers didn't even have a building. And, it wasn't because of the popularity of an erudite pastor. It was because that underneath the growth in this incipient movement was the hand of God. God was involved. It wasn't just a people thing. It wasn't some slick church growth strategy; it was beyond all that. And, again, this begs the question: Shouldn't we all accept that? Shouldn't we all see this clearly—even now in our own churches—our own ministries? This trust? This reaching out?

The sovereign hand of the Almighty was at work in the fruitfulness of this fellowship in the Book of Acts. God is truly at work, as an example to us all. We need to note that the primary protagonist in Acts is not Peter, and it's not Paul; it's the Holy Spirit. This should illustrate that our God is not a "status quo" God. God is, instead, it appears, interested in growth and expansion. God can't settle for what has been. Yes, we learn as we study the text, that 3,000 joined after one revival sermon. But, the Lord was not satisfied with that. While Peter and the rest of them may have still been "high-fiving" each other over the 3,000, the Lord remained searching for others to add to this movement. This is the God of the shepherd who searches for the one lost sheep. This is the God of the sister who sweeps the floor until she finds the lost coin. This is the God of Jesus who says, "I must go on to the next city." If it means adding another worship service, the Lord keeps adding. If it means building a new place, the Lord keeps adding. If it means you may have to give up your seat for someone, the Lord keeps adding. The highways and the hedges are not off-limits to God. The nightclubs and the street-corners are not off-limits. The Lord does whatever is necessary to keep adding. If you are content with status quo, you might not want to follow Jesus. He's always on to something new. And, THIS—this is what separates the human selfishness and unwillingness to move and to change and to trust—from God—from the Holy Spirit.

God is truly at work, as an example to us all.

IF WE WANT TO BE INCLUDED, TO WHOM DO WE REACH OUT?

When we walk with our faith, during the day or when we walk at night, do we notice the people who should be added? Do we notice those in need—maybe those who we would not normally speak to? Do we empathize and understand enough to realize that, around us, there are worthy people in need of being added to our lives, our churches? Do we step out of our comfort zone and pull people in? Do we think about saving others? Or, do we, instead, think about judging others? Think about the status quo and what might make us look good—not what God would want us to do in his example?

WHO HAS BEEN "ADDED" OR WHO IS WORTHY OF BEING "SAVED"?

In Acts, who was being added? The text tells us, it is "those who were being saved". He doesn't add them because of their money, and He doesn't add them because of their social stature. Further, we don't hear about their membership in some of the local, elitist clubs. He doesn't add them because of their academic acumen or because they seem to be the people who have it all together. In fact, if God waited to add perfect people, no one would be added! Instead, God accepted everyone—invited everyone—to His church. And, again, we have to ask ourselves, would we do the same? How often do we place a lot of weight on the school someone went to or the degree that he or she has? How many times do we allow those with the bigger house and the nice clothes, who like to tell us how much better they are than others, handle big issues at work or at school simply because of the appearance they project or the "profile" they want us to believe? And, to the contrary, how often do we not offer friendship to someone who doesn't come from "a good family" or someone who may have struggled in other ways. Many times, these are nice people eager for friendship and inclusion, and, yet, something tells us not to reach out—not to trust this relationship. And, in all truth, we often know that the well dressed, big-talker is not entirely honest or pure in his or her intentions, and we still trust him or her to show us the way. And, again, to the contrary, we often can clearly see these people who have struggled and come out on top are good people with integrity and honesty, yet… we mistrust them because of their struggle—their less than perfect lives.

In recalling the moments or times in our lives when we felt outside or excluded—maybe we were bewildered by how to belong or even how to make people happy—how to get to the next step in life regarding work or family or personal relationships—do we ever put these people who we mistrust or deem unworthy of God's favor in our place? Do we ever vow not to exclude or judge others again? Do we, instead, wonder how we might change so that we are "added" or "saved" in God's favor because of how we view others, spread fellowship and God's Word, or just try to be the best disciple we can be? I urge you, readers, to examine this in life.

Let's examine the concept that God adds those who are being saved. Those who had accepted and embraced the gift of life offered in Christ were being added, not those who showed off their money or their family connections. Those who had recognized that they could not get right with God on their own were being added. In fact, these people admitted their sinfulness and turned to the Savior. Those who had previously thought their lives weren't worth a quarter but had now been lifted by the mercies of God, were being added. Those who owned up to the fact that their goodness was insufficient and needed to rest on the righteousness of the Christ were being added. These weren't perfect people who were being added, but they were saved. Those who had the testimony that "to the utmost Jesus saves" were being added. They were "saved." Being saved has a beginning defined as the point when we are delivered from the penalty of sin (death). Being saved is a process, during which we are being delivered from the power and effects of sin (sanctification). And, finally, being saved has a conclusion, which is when we are delivered from the very presence of sin (glorification). The "saved" were those who had been rescued out of what they could not get themselves out of. The "saved" were those who had been made whole through the grace of God.

Clearly, these people were of all walks of life. They may have been the wealthy business owners that we know now—the people who golf at high-end country clubs and buy designer clothes, but… they also may be the people who struggle to put a meal on the table—a single mother looking to better herself with God—maybe a person who previously spent time on the wrong path, headed for trouble. And, we have to feel, as humans, as members of God's church, that it shouldn't be that difficult to discern between the two types of people—those who want to be saved or who are added for their merit with God as opposed to those who don't care or who wouldn't help a fellow man if he were right in front of them starving. And, when we move so quickly through our day, getting that latte in the morning, reading our paper about all the strife in the world, working hard to put a meal on our table, clothes on our kids, maybe pay for a nice vacation every summer, do we think about this? Do we think about how we are perceived or, on the other hand, how many people we may unintentionally misjudge?

READER'S PAUSE

LIVING WELL: RECALLING A MOMENT OF TRUST IN YOUR LIFE

We all have varied experiences in life and different people in our backgrounds. Today, try to recall a moment in life when you realized that you could trust someone with your best interests. Was it a teacher, a parent, or maybe an older, distant relative? Maybe you don't have one of those moments and, instead, feel that you can recall a moment when the tide turned for you on a trustworthy person. Maybe he or she showed a character flaw that surprised you or maybe someone let you down, and it was hard to get over. Can you link this to something in your present life? Maybe you can vow to include someone at work for lunch when you all go out. Or maybe you can remember to spend time with one of your children—maybe one who is in a transition period in life like entering middle school or leaving for college. Record these experiences in a journal and try to add some memories to the entry—maybe a recipe associated with a person—a photo from the past, etc.

____

____

____

____

A RETURN TO THE TEXT: WHO DO YOU SEE AS WORTHY OF BEING "ADDED" OR "SAVED"?

After reflection and upon returning to the text, when we try to picture these folks that God was adding to the church, what do we see? Do we see our current fellow churchgoers or the people in our neighborhood? We need to remember that the fact that the Lord added them to the church meant that being saved was not enough. And, again, the same rings true today. God didn't just save them; God "churched" them! Why did they need to be added? Wasn't it enough for them to just know Jesus? Wasn't it enough for them to pray at home and maybe catch a little bit of popular pastors in the media, like Joyce Meyer or Joel Osteen, on TV? They didn't really need the church did they? Did they really need the church with all those hypocrites down there? They could just read their Bibles at home and not be bothered with all that mess? Who needed institutional religion? Couldn't they just be spiritual? Religion was just man-made anyway! Right? They didn't need the church to be saved anyway!

Does this all sound familiar? How many of us have felt this way or how many people do we know who use the aforementioned justifications to get out of "being churched"—being a part of it all—accepting the good and bad—perhaps even trying to work towards a better church—one without "hypocrites" or those who feel they no longer need religion? And how does this help build community, strengthen the church, or take steps toward understanding others or understanding God? The Lord was not satisfied with them being saved; He, in fact, added them to this body of believers. It was almost automatic. If you were saved, you then needed the church. If you were saved, you were a part of the church. And it was the Lord who added them. If they didn't need the church, the Lord wouldn't have added them. He adds them because God is at work in and through the church, and the church can be the vehicle of change. There is no way to grow like God wants you to grow as a person without this body of believers. Those who God added years ago needed a church; you need a church. Church attachment is not an option; it is indispensable for those who are saved. American individualism has made us think that all we need is a relationship with Jesus as our personal Savior, and that is enough. That is not enough! You need the church. That 's why the Lord adds them. It would not be enough for the saved to go to church on the 1st and 3rd Sunday! They need to be consistent and, thereby, added as an attachment of sorts, attached to that church. Inconsistent attendance is not enough. You need attachment.

If you were saved, you were a part of the church.

SCRIPTURE REVIEW

The Lord added them to the church; He added to their number. The fact that the Lord adds to them means that God trusts this church. God wouldn't add the saved to a church, which God didn't trust. The lives of the saved mean too much. These are His children. Jesus shed His blood for these folks. The Lord purchased them. The Lord redeemed them. The Lord had taken care of them. "Saving" people cost the Father His Son, and cost the Son His life. The Lord wouldn't just trust them anywhere. The Lord puts them in the hands of the church, and the church is a steward of the saved! Parents spend time searching for a daycare for their children, because they don't want to just leave them anywhere. I was speaking to a parent recently and he was describing how intentional he was in searching out a pre-school for his child. It was taking time, because he had to find the right place. And... this is true with churches, isn't it? God adds people to churches He can trust. We align with the people we can trust; it all makes sense.

WHAT I LEARNED FROM THIS SCRIPTURE EXAMINATION, AND WHAT I'D LIKE YOU, READERS, TO LEARN–ENERGY IN ALL AREAS OF LIFE IS IMPORTANT

This concept challenged me on many fronts as a member of a church and as a pastor of a church. I started asking myself some difficult questions: Can God trust our church enough to add to it? Can God trust that people will be cared for? Can God trust that people will not be discriminated against because of their unique personalities, race, gender, physical challenges, and social status? Can God trust that outsiders will not be relegated to the margins of society? Can God trust that efficient, vibrant new-members ministries will be in place for those who join? Can God trust that the leadership will be faithful in follow up with those whom the Lord sends? Can the Lord trust that church will be as excited about developing new members as they are getting new members? God will not add to a church that God does not trust! And we can understand that, can't we? After all, we have all had our trust issues, and we have all put trust in the wrong people or not trusted those we should. It is complicated, but it shouldn't be.

Energy in all areas of life is important.

We touched on relationships earlier. And, regarding the text, what was it about this body of people that led God to trust it enough to add to it? The Lord was confident in this church. In the words of the late preacher of London, John R.W. Stott, "the Lord was confident in this church because of its relationships!" This church had the right RELATIONSHIP WITH THE APOSTLE'S IN LEARNING. The very first thing said about this church was "they devoted themselves to the apostles' teaching…" I wonder; what was the first thing said about your church? Before there is any discussion about how big their budget is—before there is any discussion about how many services they have—the very first thing said was that this church was dedicated to learning the word passed down through their teachers. They had a relationship of submission to the apostles and, particularly, to the Word passed down through the Apostles. These relationships that I had you recall and reflect on earlier? These relationships to this church were inherent to their success, their understanding of God and His trust in them.

This church was still burning from the fire of Pentecost. They were shouting from Pentecost, but they shouted themselves right on to the church school and the mid-week Bible study. Go ahead and shout, but shout yourself right to the classroom. In Christian discipleship, fire and experience are not enough. Shouting is not enough. The feel-good experience of Sunday morning was not enough. Moments of enthusiasm are not sufficient in order to make it as a child of God. People from other movements are able to confuse us, because some of us have fire but not substance—burning but no learning. It was Martin King who once said, "Some folks have more religion in their hands and feet than they do in their hearts, heads, and souls." So just as with this original church, the fervor and fire of Pentecost was not enough for them to make it through everything they would have to go through we need depth—just as they needed depth. Depth came through the Word. Energy without depth is no good!

We all put energy into certain components of our lives—creating a warm home for our families, working to get to a certain position at work or even working towards a fitness goal in the gym. Do we always put forth our best efforts concerning our energy, however? Do we stand up for friends—do we go the extra mile when a promotion is not on the table—do we spread the Word of God? We all enjoy fellowship, but do we work or put energy towards spreading it, including others, doing the work of God to be "added" or "saved" by God in the bigger sense of both words? Not always, but we are capable.

Actually, learning fuels the fire. Truth is like lighter fluid. Truth is like hot coals, which sustain the fire. Your fire will go out if there is nothing to sustain it. Your fire can't help but to be ignited when you learn about the sustaining, sanctifying, saving grace of God. Your fire can't help but to but be reignited when you learn about Jesus being your advocate and your high priest. Truth feeds the fire. Your shout will be more enjoyable when it is fed by truth. And, truth, as we discussed and explored before, is up to us.

This original church continued steadfastly in the Apostle's doctrine. This is the teaching passed down to the apostles by Jesus about Jesus. This wasn't the latest fad in inspirational instruction; this was the Christo-centric instruction, which focused on the Gospel. At the heart of the Gospel is Jesus Christ. The right thing was being taught in this church. There was no self-help stuff being taught here. The Apostles were not giving motivational talks; they were teaching the truth about Christ. How I wish we got as excited about the truth of Christ as we do about current events! God does not mind adding to church where the Gospel of Christ is being taught and preached. Any church that has become bored with Jesus is in trouble, because God can't add to that. The Lord can't add to a church that has become uncomfortable with the cross. The Lord can't trust a church that has issues with the blood of the Lamb. The Lord can't trust a church that compromises the core of the Gospel in order to draw a crowd. That is a church, which might be drawing a crowd, but the Lord is not adding to that. The Lord knows, and we know, that truth in relationships—with God—with others—is key. You are not open to learning and open to love if you don't trust.

The Lord can't add to a church that has become uncomfortable with the cross.

What was it about this church that made God trust it enough to add to it? Not only was it its relationship with the Apostles in learning, but it was also its RELATIONSHIPS WITH EACH OTHER IN CARING. Not only did they continue in the apostle's doctrine, but also they continued it in fellowship. They didn't just learn the Word, but they actualized it through how they dealt with each other. Learning was not just some cerebral activity; it was a means to the ends of being able to embody what they learned. People get so excited about revelation in God's word; revelation should impact relationship. Don't tell me how smart you are, but at the same time you can't get along with anyone! Don't tell me how much Bible you know, but can't speak to certain folks. Recalling that day that started with the latte earlier—that we tried to recall in our busy, busy lives... Did we try to talk to anyone new? Do we ever trust and reach out unconditionally? This is what God wants us to do.

KOINONIA: WHEN FELLOWSHIP IS MORE THAN JUST "PUNCH AND COOKIES" WITH FRIENDS

So this original church was a place where they cared about each other. Fellowship meant more than punch and cookies. Fellowship meant more than the decorations at holiday parties or, again, that tendency to like or to trust and follow those who look like they're rich or powerful. Fellowship meant sharing with each other—with everyone. Fellowship meant some money and not just money to show off. They sold property and possessions in order to be able to give to those who had need. It might sound radical to us, and I don't necessarily recommend this practice for the contemporary church, but we can give back on occasion. We can remember that even if we struggle and work on, we have more than the homeless or the hungry. In fact, I recommend the mindset. The mindset is most important and says, "we will do what we have to—to make sure the people are taken care of!" Fellowship meant sacrificing for each other to make sure everyone is taken care of. This group of people recognized that all of them would have seasons when they needed some help. Just because you were "riding high" now didn't mean that day wouldn't come when you found yourself in need of some help. Some of our politicians and leaders often arrogantly ignore those who need help or naively believe that they or someone they know will never be in need. We know better. Those of us who trust in God and each other and love and reach out in fellowship—we know that everyone's time of need may come, and we are ready.

The word for fellowship is "koinonia". This word has to do with what you share "in common with someone." And we all know this, don't we? These folks of this original church "shared in" something. They shared in a common relationship with Christ. They were from diverse backgrounds. They were from different places. They spoke different languages. But, they were suddenly all a unit. This is the miracle of Pentecost. The miracle of Pentecost was koinonia. "Fellowship was born on Pentecost." The miracle of Pentecost was not speaking in tongues; it was unity. Nothing could bring them together like the Spirit. Nothing can bring us together like the Spirit of God. Through the Spirit they recognized that they shared in something. They shared in a common connection to Christ. Because they shared in, they were able to share with. Their intense trusting relationship with God —or vertical to the heavens—lead to close, warm relationships with each other—or horizontal as they made their ways through their, presumably busy days, just as we experience now. What we share "in" should help us with "sharing with." If you are connected to Christ, you will be connected to me. You can't brag about how much I love the Lord, and yet walk on the other side of the church so that you don't have to speak. The quality of your vertical relationship with God is measured by the quality of your horizontal relationship with people. If you can't love the people, you don't love God! If you say you love God and hate your brother or sister, you are lying! The Lord could trust this church, because there was some caring going on. He could send some new folks here and expect that this church was going to look out for them. He could expect that no one was going to be ignored. The Lord doesn't mind sending folks to a place where they will be more than a number!

What made God trust this church to the point where He added to it daily those who were being saved? It was their relationship with the apostles in learning; it was their relationship with each other in caring but it was also THEIR RELATIONSHIP WITH THE WORLD IN WITNESSING. The fact that the Lord was adding to their numbers daily—for those who were being saved, it meant that there were more people being saved—more people and the church was still growing and learning. The fact that there were some people being saved means that those who were already saved were sharing the news with the world. The Lord could not add anyone to the church if the church was not doing its job in reaching the world. Adding folks to the church was a cooperative effort between God and the church. God could only add the folks that the church could reach. The adding to the church was not a passive effort solely in the hands of God; the church itself had a role.

WHAT DID THE CHURCH IN THE TEXT HEAR THAT WE, IN OUR OWN CHURCHES, NEED TO HEAR?

These folks had heard Jesus when He said in His parting words "and you shall receive power after that the Holy Ghost is come upon you; and you shall be witnesses unto me in…" These people, as limited as they may have been, were committed to getting the Word out. The Lord saved them, and they were enjoying their salvation. But, salvation is not just meant to be enjoyed; it is meant to be shared. The news they had was too good for them to keep to themselves. They had to share it. Jesus died, so they had to share it! Jesus was raised, and they had to share that. Jesus ascended, and they absolutely had to share it. Jesus would be returning, and they had to share that as well.

God could trust them, because they were not a self-contained body. There was an element of outreach. They wanted others to share in their programs and their fellowship. I recall a story about an oil refinery once told to me. A man visited an oil refinery, and after being shown all of the intricate systems and equipment, he asked the tour guide "where's the shipping department? Where's the place that the oil is shipped out to benefit other people?" The tour guide said, "There is no shipping department. All the oil we produce and refine is used to keep the refinery going." This original church was not like that, and we can't be like that. We have to reach out in fellowship—we have to trust—in order for God to trust us. God adds to the church when He trusts, and those worthy of trust have opened their hearts, minds, churches, and homes to others—as disciples of God and leaders in fellowship.

God adds to the church when He trusts.

2

SOMETHING ABOUT THAT NAME

ALLOWING TOLERANCE IN LIFE

NOW THAT WE TRUST, CAN WE BE TOLERANT?

Now, we've established that it is truly difficult to trust and open our hearts to others. And, it is just as difficult to accept some of the more mysterious components of God's love for us—specifically, that He will add, save, and love people in His favor as He sees fit. Further, we may not know why or how He evaluates any of us; we will just have to accept who He chooses and when He decides to make clear to us what mission or life's goals He expects from us. Often, we expect things of ourselves that don't come to fruition until well after we have planned. Also, we often observe others that we may not see as valuable or relevant to us, but God has a plan for him or her, and we need to be accepting of that plan. Further even more so, we need to learn to trust in others and to love unconditionally. We need to accept God's favor and open our own hearts to others. Surely, we know that people are different than us, but we need to keep open hearts and open minds to all people.

We need to accept God's favor and open our own hearts to others.

A TRIP TO TOLERANCE

One of the most memorable parts of my trip to Turkey one year was a visit to a place called "The Garden of Tolerance," located in the region of Antalya. Located in this Garden of Tolerance are a Christian church, a mosque, and a synagogue. These houses of worship were located right next to each other. These worship places were so close together that in a matter of moments you could walk from one building to the other. A priest led worship services at the church, a rabbi led at the synagogue, and an Imam led prayers at the mosque. It was amazing to see these different faith traditions in such close proximity. The Garden of Tolerance is intended to symbolize the necessity of peace, respect, and appreciation of these major world religions, as well as the real possibility that these faith traditions can meaningfully exist in close proximity. And, this tolerance and co-existence don't always pop into our minds, first. In fact, most often, we notice the differences first.

For all of us, readers, we know that we often interact with people of different nationalities, ethnicities, and faiths. Are we always tolerant, however? Do we always try to understand who or what we have encountered when faced with a new religion, a new way of life, or even something as simple as a new food or clothing specific to an area of the world where we've never been? I don't think we do as much as we should. Just as we discussed earlier in the previous chapter the idea that, we expect a lot from God or others, but do we ever get to know others or remain inclusive and celebratory when we have to branch out and be a disciple—help God look for lost sheep and people who need our help? We will discuss here the fact that, while we may like travel and talking about other religions or working with people of other ethnicities and faiths, do we ever really get to know what makes them tick or what they believe and understand to be true? What do we have in common? What can we do to get to know one another better?

In many circles, there is an emphasis on tolerance and appreciation of differences. Across the world, there is this effort to bring together people of different races, ethnicities, and religions to the table for the sake of tolerance. Inter-racial, inter-religious, commissions are actively engaged in bringing people together. Right now in Jackson, Mississippi, there is a group called "Mission Mississippi", which is an interdenominational and multiracial religious organization that has gotten participating restaurants to give multiracial parties 22% discounts on their bills. Efforts like this one have become popular in some areas of the United States.

We live in a society, which is becoming more diverse by the moment.

This ecumenical spirit of religious tolerance and appreciation is to be applauded, because so much harm has been done throughout history because of intolerance and bigotry. Discrimination, terrorism, "ethnic" cleansing, and so on have occurred, because people can't deal with other people who are different than they are. The sense of group superiority has had tragic consequences in the human community. We live in a society, which is becoming more diverse by the moment. You will have big problems if you can't handle people who believe differently than you do—or look different, eat differently, speak differently, and act differently.

But, as much as we applaud the emphasis on tolerance and as necessary as it is to appreciate and respect the religious beliefs of others, the Christian church cannot be shy, sheepish, or bashful about it's confidence in and declaration of the name of Jesus. Tolerance does not mean compromise. It dishonors the name of Christ to disrespect or discriminate against folks of other faiths in the name of Jesus. It dishonors the name of Christ to fanatically "beat people over the head" with Jesus talk. But, it also dishonors the name of Christ if we are hesitant about declaring His name. In some Christian circles, theological schools, and churches accentuating the "name of Jesus" is discouraged so that no one is offended. Christians have become nervous about praying in the name of Jesus in so-called ecumenical settings. Some churches or "ministries" have stopped putting so much emphasis on Jesus in order to attract a larger and more diverse following. The bottom-line is that some Christians have become ashamed of the name of Jesus.

THE EARLY CHURCH'S TAKE ON TOLERANCE

The early church and these preachers in this incipient movement called, simply, the church" were not bashful about the name of Jesus. At the center of their message is the fact that Jesus was crucified, but He was raised from the dead. That was the throbbing heart of their message.

There was no compromising of that, even when they stood in the face of danger.

You can't expect to be favored by God and not be opposed by the enemy.

Everything was going so well for this early Christian church that we have so deeply examined in the previous chapter. The church was growing; lives were being changed. The Lord was adding to the church those who were being saved, because He trusted this church. He trusted them, because it was a learning church, it was a fellowshipping church, it was a witnessing church, and it was a worshipping church. But, as they were growing in mission, they were also growing in opposition. Mission and opposition grew in tandem. Blessing and trouble often grow in tandem. As God was favoring them, they were being opposed by the devil. Those two often happen in tandem. You can't expect to be favored by God and not be opposed by the enemy. The wheat of blessing and growth grows in tandem with the tares of opposition and resistance. Divine favor makes you a target for satanic attack. Keeping this divine favor and association in mind—your love of Jesus or your commitment to Him—will make you a target for those who want to test you, but this fortitude will also make you strong in the face of it all. When your faith is tested, you can be ready. When you say the name "Jesus" in prayer, in daily life, and in daily mission, you are strong in your faith and able to talk about it, stave off Satan, and live strong and happy with God. As we said at the beginning of this chapter, other faiths can live in harmony—other faiths can talk about their God and their belief and still know that you are strong in yours as well.

Other faiths can talk about their God and their belief and still know that you are strong in yours as well.

OUR SCRIPTURE REFERENCE

In Acts 4:8-12, Peter and John were on their way to the temple at the hour of prayer. As they are on their way, they run into a crippled man at the gate called "Beautiful." Someone put him there every day so that he could beg for a living. In the words of the late preacher and author, Dr. E.K. Bailey, "This man had a serious defect with caused him to have a sad dependence." As Peter and John approach him, he began to beg for money. Peter, after the man had fixed his eyes on them expecting to receive something from them, informed the man that they didn't have any "spare change." However, Peter goes beyond what the man requests and gets at the heart of the need. "Silver and gold we don't have, but what we do have we give to you. In the name of Jesus Christ get up and walk." The man got up, like a young gazelle, walking for the first time. He went to church with Peter and John and began jumping and shouting. This behavior, of course, drew a crowd.

As Peter is explaining what happened to the crowd, some of the Jewish authorities walk up and, disturbed by what they are hearing from Peter and John, they seize them and put them in jail for the night. The establishment is worried, because this message about Christ is changing things. The order is being turned upside down. People are being liberated. The establishment is not always comfortable with that. Therefore, the next morning, Peter and John are brought before the Sanhedrin court. As they are standing there, the court begins to question them: "By what authority or name did you do this?" By "this", they are referring to the healing of this cripple man. By all indications, the healed man was standing right there with them. The Sanhedrin court points to this healed man and asks, "how did this happen?"

In the face of these brilliant legal minds and theological scholars, Peter responds. He doesn't have much going for him at this moment except for one thing: "then Peter, filled with the Holy Spirit...." The only thing Peter has to stand up in the midst of this hostile environment is the Spirit of God. That's all he has, but that's all he needs. For the Spirit will give him what he needs to say at that moment. The Spirit of God gives him courage and content right at that moment. The Spirit of God tells him what to say and gives him the strength to say it. If you would just stand, the Spirit will stand up in you at the right moment! In intimidating circumstances, the Spirit of God will stand up in you and give you courage and content.

When Peter commences his defense, he hits them with a bit of irony. He says, in essence, "Are we being brought up on charges of for being kind to a cripple man?" And then he goes on to respond to their inquiry. They want to know by what name or authority this has happened; Peter has no problem telling them. In doing so, Peter actually stands up for the name of Christ in the midst of a hostile environment. This is the challenge for the church. This is the challenge for the child of God. Can you stand up for the name of Christ in hostile environments? Anyone can talk about Jesus in Sunday school. Anyone can testify about him in prayer meeting. It's easy for me to own Christ in the comfortable confines of this worship place. But what about outside of here? Will you own Christ in a world where owning Christ is offensive? Will you own Christ, and risk being called narrow-minded? Will you own Christ and risk being politically incorrect? Will you own Christ when it might cost you something? Will you own Christ when it might cost you?

Peter stands up and says there are some things you and all of Israel need to know about Christ and His precious name. Concerning Jesus, Peter says that He is the SOURCE OF THE BLESSING. It is by the name of Jesus of Nazareth that this has happened. In case they weren't sure who this Jesus was, Peter tells them "this is the Jesus whom you crucified, but God raised." You had one plan for Jesus, but God did something else. You killed him, but God raised him. What they did could not hold him down. What God did "overrode" what they did. The enemy was in charge of Friday, but God took control of Sunday morning. They were active on Friday, but God was active on Sunday morning. In case they didn't know the One by whom this happened, Peter clears up His Identity.

IS THIS A MIRACLE? WHAT DO WE LEARN FROM THIS SCRIPTURE?

Yes, something did happen. This man was cured. Peter says that the means by which he was healed is the name of Jesus. Peter was the one who reached out his hand to the man, but the power was not in Peter's hand. Nothing happened to this crippled man until Peter invoked the name of Jesus. When Peter called on the name of Jesus, the man received strength in his leg, and it ran down into his ankle, and he was able to get up. There is something about that name. This is why we can't be ashamed of that name. Things begin to happen when we call on that name. This is why we can't be bashful about declaring that name. When he called on the name of Jesus, everything associated with the name came to fore. To invoke the name of Jesus is to summon all the healing power of the Lord. To call on the name of Jesus is to release into my circumstances the power associated with His person. If there is healing in Christ it comes to the fore when you call on that name. If there is possibility in that name, it comes running to the fore when you call on that name. Things happen when you call on the name. Demons tremble at that name. Principalities become nervous at that name. Disease becomes uneasy at that name. Everything that we find daunting or upsetting can become uneasy or go away with this name. All that upsets us can become something that simply challenges us with this name. All that we fear or find threatening will change if we commit to keeping that name—Jesus—with us at all times—in our hearts, in our minds, and on our tongues—in constant conversation and prayer about Him.

READER'S PAUSE

LIVING WELL: STANDING UP TO THE NAYSAYERS

Have you ever felt uncomfortable or that you should clarify something or stand up to someone who is wrong but you feel either intimidated or embarrassed? Have you watched someone stop a bullying incident or succinctly defeat a bully who has directed his hostility his or her way? How did any of this make you feel? If you could do it again, would you change your reaction?

____

____

____

Did you ever oppose somebody on an important point and feel good about yourself? Or—have you ever seen someone get very angry when he or she was opposed or argued with?

____

____

____

____

Recall one of these incidents or picture it happening now and come up with a personal mission statement that addresses, specifically, how you feel about your strong personal beliefs and credos. In other words, how do you live your life? Record this in a journal and reflect on how it makes you feel—proud, nervous, defensive, strong, etc.

Take this message to your next social interaction. Treat the person you encounter with that credo in mind—make a point to ask how he or she is—tell him or her that God loves him or her—ask about his or her plans for the day.

HOW CAN YOU LIVE IN PETER'S EXAMPLE?

And, in getting back to someone who did stand up for his beliefs, we examine Peter, who, as he is being questioned, reveals that Jesus is the source of the healing. The healing has come by means of the name of the Christ. I'm sure these Jewish leaders were perplexed. They thought they had gotten rid of Jesus. When Jesus was walking around, they had problems with His healing. Some of His healing occurred on the Sabbath day, and they had issues with that. Many of His healings drew large crowds. Jesus caused a commotion with some of his healings. They thought He was off the scene. But, here, Peter was implying that the One they all thought they got rid of is still causing trouble. These authorities were probably saying, "We still have to deal with Him." The name of Jesus could perform the same thing that the person of Jesus performed when He was here. Jesus still causes trouble when we call on His name. They thought He was gone. They did not know that Christ was just as present as ever. They did not know that Jesus was still around. Peter knew what we should now—that "He's not dead; He's yet alive". Jesus is alive in His people then—and He is alive now. And when His people own His name, Jesus can cause as much trouble—as much proactive change—now as He did when He was walking around in the flesh. Knowing Jesus is knowing change and forward movement in faith. We need to facilitate that at all times—understand our role in keeping His name associated with our faith and our direction and motivation for doing all that is good in this world.

To hit this home—in his little mini-sermon, Peter shows that he is not ashamed of the name of Jesus, and he declares that Jesus is the source of the blessing. But, then he declares that Jesus is the STONE WHICH HAS BEEN REJECTED. "He is" said Peter, "the stone you builders rejected, which had become the cornerstone…" Peter uses language concerning Jesus, which is familiar in the New Testament. According to 1 Peter 2:4, Jesus is the precious cornerstone. According to Ephesians 2:20, Jesus is the chief cornerstone. According to this text, Jesus is the rejected cornerstone. All of this may be based on a Christian appropriation of the metaphor used in Psalm 118:22: "the stone which the builders rejected, has become the cornerstone." Scholars will all agree here that, regardless of how the stone is interpreted here—rejected, accepted, or the source of all blessings—Jesus is our cornerstone in faith. And that is a good metaphor on which to build our own faith—our own tolerance and acceptance of whatever has been presented to us. Jesus is our stone; we can be His in exclaiming His name and defending our beliefs to others.

JESUS AS "THE STONE" IN LIFE

In this sermon, Peter declares that Jesus is the stone, which the people rejected. But, this same One whom they rejected is the One whom God has made the cornerstone. The stone, which has been ignored, is now the cornerstone. The cornerstone was crucial in the construction of a building. The cornerstone was set at the corner of the foundation of a building. This stone served at least two purposes. It would help to solidify the foundation so that the rest of the building could be built on top of it. The cornerstone would also help to make sure the rest of the building was level. The cornerstone was set in a level fashion and actually established the balance for the rest of the building. If the cornerstone were off, so would be the rest of the building.

Peter says "as crucial as the cornerstone is the building, so is Jesus to life." This is why Peter could not be ashamed of His name. Jesus is too critical to the construction of life. These authorities were builders of the people. They were integral in building the nation of Israel, and they sought to do it without the cornerstone, which is Jesus. They not only ignored the cornerstone; they actually rejected it. They looked at it and acted like they didn't need it. I wonder how many of us are trying to build life without Jesus as the cornerstone. Jesus holds life together. Jesus helps to balance everything else out. If you try to build without Him, things tend to fall apart. In the midst of life's craziness, Jesus helps to hold it together. Some of us have been able to stand the test of time, because we've had the right cornerstone. We've been through some things, which should have brought you down by now, but we're standing because of the cornerstone. Make sure the stone—whatever it is—is set in the right place. Jesus will make sure everything else is making some kind of sense. This is why we can't be ashamed of Him. This is why we can't be hesitant to declare His name. He is to life what the cornerstone is to the building!

Peter stands there in front of this intimidating body of people—of bullies—and he remains standing up for Christ. In doing so, he declares that Jesus is the source of the blessing. He goes on to say that Jesus is the stone, which has been rejected. And finally he declares that Jesus is the SAVIOR WHO IS UNIQUE. Peter moves from explaining what has happened to declaring a central truth. Without apology, Peter says, "salvation is found in no one else." It sounds too narrow; it sounds too "old school". But, this is what Peter believes. "Salvation," is in no one else! "Salvation," that is to say "the process by which God makes us whole." "Salvation," that is the experience in which God rescues us. We are in need of rescue—rescue from our sin—rescue from our guilt—rescue from our purposelessness—rescue from our self-centeredness. All of that is one person: Jesus!

PUTTING MORALITY ON TRIAL

Peter moves from defense to appeal. He is not simply describing how this thing happened; he actually challenges the very leaders who have him on trial. He puts them on trial by declaring, "For there is no other name under heaven given among people by which we must be saved." By saying "we," he is including the folks to whom he is speaking. He says this is the name, which has healed this crippled man, but, if the truth were told, this is the same name by which you need to be saved. The court doesn't even know it, but now they are on trial. Peter appeals to them to embrace this name. He says to the Supreme Court, "you need to be saved." He says, "I know you are the law of the land, but you need to be saved. I know you are the religious scholars, but you need to be saved. I know you are public figures, but you need to be saved. I know you are the embodiment of high moral standards, but you need to be saved." The fact that Peter says this to them means that Peter is confident that Jesus is able to save even them. He says, "There is no other name under heaven by which we must be saved." "We," in this case, includes them. Peter has already seen what Jesus can do for a beggar. He's confident that Jesus can do the same for a "baller." Bringing it present day, these brothers on the basketball court—these men we look up to for the athletic prowess these days—the Lebron Jameses—the Kobe Bryants—are in as much need of what Jesus offers as the man who is begging for money. Whether at the gate begging or on the bench handing down decisions and acting as examples to all, they were and are all in need of what Jesus has to offer. The salvation of Christ is not just for the privileged; it is also for the common man and woman. The salvation of Christ is not just for the addict hanging out on the corner; it is also for the executive in the boardroom. For all these people, the message is the same "there is no other name given among people, by which..." No matter where life takes you—a world of celebrity—a life of hard work—a life in service to God—Jesus is the reason for our success and our need for faith and for love beyond our worldly possessions.

They, like the rest of us, are seeking salvation and are beholden to Jesus for it.

IN CHAPTER ONE–AND NOW IN CHAPTER TWO –WE'RE STILL TALKING ABOUT SALVATION!

This "salvation", this wholeness is in His "name." Getting right with God is in the name of Jesus. The name of Abraham Lincoln is often associated with Emancipation, but there is no salvation in that name. The name of Martin King might bring about inspiration, but there's no salvation in that name. The name Barack Obama might bring about motivation for some seeking to accomplish their goals, but there's no salvation in that name. There is motivation—there is pride—there is aspiration, but... there is no salvation. They, like the rest of us, are seeking salvation and are beholden to Jesus for it.

Even the enemy is aware of the possibilities in the name of Jesus.

This is why Peter and John keep declaring that name. After Peter speaks to the court, the court recesses and caucuses amongst themselves. They admit that they can't deny the miracle, but they can issue a "gag-order". They tell Peter and John "we don't mind you preaching. And we don't mind you healing. Above all, we don't mind you having church... but please don't do it in the name of Jesus." Even the enemy is aware of the possibilities in the name of Jesus. The enemy doesn't mind me getting up and giving motivational talks with a grin painted on my face. The enemy does not mind me telling nice stories about my family—as long as I don't preach in that name. And this is powerful. This transcends, again, what all these powerful men—the Obamas, the Lincolns, the Kings—can do for us. It makes us like them—waiting for salvation for Jesus—certain that we need to speak His name to get that fortitude behind us.

3

UNEXPECTED ALLIES

ACCEPTING AND LEARNING TO LIVE WITH SUCCESS IN OUR DAILY LIVES

YES—WE'RE STILL TALKING ABOUT SUCCESS

Success is sometimes hard to explain. It is difficult to understand why some people, some movements, and some ideas end up being successful. It is even hard to fathom how some ministries explode the way they do. And many times, we want to know just that very answer so that we might employ the same strategies and ideas in our own lives and ministries, which, apparently, led to success. As reasonable humans, we believe in cause and effect; therefore, there has to be some observable, quantifiable reasons why a particular person, business, idea, or ministry has met with unique success. We hear success stories, and we want to know, "how did they do it?" Pastors and church leaders attend seminars and workshops given by "successful" ministries in order to discover what it is that leads to success. We read books trying to figure how some folks have achieved what they have in order to attempt to duplicate it.

Success is sometimes hard to explain.

As much as we want to know the secrets to success, prosperity, and the respect that often accompanies all of it, the truth is simply that sometimes there is no logical explanation as to why certain people, movements, ministries, companies, and ideas end up being successful. When certain ministries or churches are asked how they have experienced so much growth, they will attribute it to one thing or another, often stumped by their own success and the reasons for it. But, there is often an explanation, which goes unnoticed and unspoken, and that is simply the "hand of God." When the hand of God is on a particular person, movement, or church, no one can always explain why it's working. This is especially the case when that person, movement, or ministry doesn't really have what we think it takes to make it work. After all, we all hear those stories about underdogs and unlikely success stories in daily life: The woman who created her own cookie empire based on her destitute grandmother's recipe or that six year old who raised more for cancer awareness than larger charities all through a simple lemonade stand! What we are not aware of, sometimes, is that God's presence and favor on you or your project often compensates for what you don't have. There is no way that some of us would be where we are or doing what we're doing if it weren't for the hand of God. Sometimes, that is the only way to explain what is happening in your life or in the lives and ministries of others. Often, too, understanding this helps us understand our own struggles and rewards and the feelings of others when they seem to begrudge others success or get jealous in some way.

Once we rectify this concept personally, it is easier to see the concept in others and in the church. It is also easier to take the lessons we see, read, and learn from, and apply it to our own lives. Regarding the early church that we examined in previous chapters, the only way to explain the growth, vigor and vitality in that institution is to credit the hand of God. Sociologically, economically, and politically, they never had what it takes to succeed. And… we can't explain it, can we? The sociologists and church growth gurus would not be able to make sense of what this band of believers experienced in the book of Acts. It can only be the hand of God. In the face of limited resources, this church kept thriving, and in the face of some seeds of internal discord, they kept thriving. Even in the face of external opposition, they kept thriving. You can only explain all of this as the hand of God. Is it difficult for us to consider, modern day, that a group of people with no money, with some confusion and discord regarding how to do things, and even with some form of ignorance and naiveté present, would thrive and become an example to others? Yes, it is very difficult for us to fathom. After all, we live in a society where hard work is not always rewarded and, it appears, that faith is not always present in success. Perhaps we should consider the fact that we do not always know the whole story. Good people often have illness in the family or financial trouble, and people who we perceive to be troubled or difficult—not deserving of success and happiness—do enjoy success. Again, we have to examine the fact that the old saying may be true: "God only gives you what you handle" After all, people are stronger than they appear, and… people who are difficult may have endured tremendous strife in their lives before finding success.

CHECKING IN WITH THE "EARLY CHURCH" AGAIN

Again, with this early church—this unlikely group of successful heroes—we find growth and success. This group is not comprised of the "Talented Tenth;" these are the common people who are populating this movement. This incipient movement is mobilized around the idea that their "hero," a Galilean peasant, was crucified and then was raised from the dead! Really? Around that idea, this movement actually blossomed like a rose in the desert. The only way to make sense out of it is that the hand of the Lord was on them. The hand of the Lord represents something that is, as we established, often hard for us to explain or understand—especially present day.

We are all familiar with this sense of divine favor, and this sense of divine leaning is particularly evident in chapters four and five of Acts. In these chapters, the opposition intensifies. The enemy gets busy. Trouble rises. Sometimes you don't know how much the Lord is on your side until trouble rises. Sometimes you are not aware of how much God's hand is upon you until the enemy gets active. God shows himself strong when life has made you weak. God shows himself to be a provider when life has taken some things away from you. Gods' hand is on this sect of believers called the way, and it shows itself, amongst other things, in the form of an unexpected ally. This is definitely a concept that we can bring present day in perspective.

OUR SCRIPTURE REFERENCE

Let's recall: In Acts 5:33-40, the first time Peter and John stood before the Sanhedrin court, they were told not to preach or teach in the name of

Jesus anymore. The authorities were afraid of that name. Even the enemy knew there was power in that name. Even the enemy knew that things happen in that name. They had seen that a crippled man was healed in that name. Therefore the authorities said to these unlearned preachers, "We don't mind you preaching and teaching. You can preach all over town. You can give all types of motivational and inspirational messages, but please don't do it in the name of Jesus! Please don't heal in that name!" And, as we established in the previous chapter in our examination of the power of that name, they were so bold as to speak it again. And in our observation of this brave act, it becomes apparent that you know you have power when the enemy is that afraid of just the name. Their only recourse is to stop them, because they have no other reasonable retort.

In the text, the apostles are released, and they go right back to doing what they were told not to do. For this, they are jailed again by the authorities, yet God intervenes and liberates them from prison. And, they go right back to doing the same thing—preaching what they believe—bravely spreading the word of Jesus. The authorities find out, apprehend them, and bring them before the High Priest. By this time the Jewish authorities have had enough. The high priest says to them, "we gave you strict orders not to teach in this name.... yet you have filled Jerusalem with your teaching and are determined to make us guilty of this man's blood." Peter responds, and it is then that we read of the INTENTION OF THE ENEMY. "When they hear this, they are furious and want to put them to death." Literally, "when they hear this, their hearts are cut in half..." "When they heard this..." What did they hear which could have made them so irritated? What bothered them so much? What did Peter say? It may not surprise you because, as we've discussed here, success and a happy life are determined, in large part, by your faith and, almost with fail, by the Hand of God.

Loyalty to God first and success and happiness will follow.

What we know is that Peter tells them of his loyalty to Christ. "Yes, you told us not to preach in that name", says Peter. "However, if it is a matter of us obeying you or obeying God, we choose the latter." The authorities, the governing body, told them not to speak in that name. But as much as the apostles respected the authorities, they couldn't concede to or cooperate with this policy. Peter explains that their loyalty is to God first. And—isn't this how we should all conduct our lives? Loyalty to God first and success and happiness will follow.

Now, what else did Peter say? Peter actually reminded them that, for their feelings and persecution of him, they were the enemies of Christ. "You killed Jesus by hanging him on a cross..." Peter put it right in their faces that they were directly responsible for the death of Jesus. And, then, he declares the victory of Christ: "The God of our ancestors raised Jesus from the dead." Jesus overcame what you did to Him. The Sadducees in the crowd would have been infuriated by this, because they did not believe in the resurrection. And this is all true. Jesus did overcome. There were people angry, and there were men of conviction, like Peter and the apostles, leading the way to Jesus' word despite threats to harm them and jail them—even ostracize them. It is this fortitude that, often, in our present day struggles with world war and poverty and racism and hunger—that we need to call on to be the best we can be—to live in Peter's example—in Jesus' example—the way God wants us to.

What we don't often consider present day is the divinity and royalty that Peter brings to the table next. Peter does go on to tell them of the royalty of Christ. "God exalted Him to His own right side as Prince and Savior that He might bring Israel to repentance and forgive their sins." This same Jesus, whom they crucified because they believed He violated the laws of God by breaking Sabbath codes and so forth, has now been vindicated by His elevation to God's right hand. These theologians and public officials can't take it, and finally Peter tells them of the ministry of Christ. He says that they have been called to be witnesses of these things, and that he and the apostles plan to continue telling the story.

"When they heard this..." This is all they needed to hear. Their hearts were "sawn in two..." They decided that these brothers had to die. The authorities couldn't discourage the apostles by imprisoning them, and they couldn't stop them by beating them. They couldn't stop them even by threatening them, so they decided that the only way to stop them was to kill them. And, readers, know this: You know you have defeated the enemy when the enemy has to resort to simply bullying you. They have lost at the table of reason. They have lost at the table of argument. They have lost at the table of undeniable impact, so they have to resort to getting rid of you. They have to resort to force. When somebody resorts to just plain old force against you, that's how you know you have defeated that bully. When all this person, this opposing force, can do is talk about you, you know you have won. And, as we said before, when all they can do is try to destroy you, you know you have won. Your enemy has reached the end of the rope. This is absolutely something we need to strive to remember in our daily lives: Our fortitude and resolve will eventually be rewarded. Any ill will we feel against us will not last and is born of jealousy and defeat.

READER'S PAUSE

LIVING WELL: ENJOYING SUCCESS AND UNDERSTANDING FEAR AND JEALOUSY

Can you detail your idea of success? Can you put into words where you see yourself when you picture absolute happiness and success? Record this in your journal and, with it, list the steps you might take to achieve such greatness.

___

___

___

Now, can you also recall when you were tested? When the world felt empty or too challenging? Do you have any fears—any regrets? List these too.

___

___

___

___

Now, reflect on and record your thoughts on people who have helped you or maybe, to the contrary, people who should have helped you but didn't.

Note this and move on. Your success is still at the top of your list.

CONTACT WELLS FARGO BANK WITH ANY NAME/ADDRESS CHANGES

NUMBER OF PADS ☐4 ☐2 ☐1 NEW VINYL COVER ☐ STARTING NUMBER ➡ 250

DIANNA DORSEY ALLEN
DETRA V MARSHALL
1089 N MERIDIAN AVE
SAN BERNARDINO, CA 92410-1033

Current Check Style **WD-PDWAF**

Indicate new check style here ____________

15121664073395

16-24/1220 4399
0623333416

Harland Clarke

To Reorder Checks, Verify Shipping Status and Review Previous Order History:

Sign on at **wellsfargo.com/checks**

- OR -

Call Us At **1-800-TO-WELLS** (1-800-869-3557)

WELLS FARGO

Wells Fargo Bank, N.A.
California
wellsfargo.com

⑆122000247⑆ 0623333416⑈

Routing and Transit Number | Account Number

REORDER FORM

WHEN YOU ARE LOYAL TO GOD, WILL SUCCESS AND HAPPINESS IMMEDIATELY FOLLOW?

What the authorities heard from these perceived "rebels" should have led them to change. It's interesting that, after Peter preached his first sermon, in which he said some of the same things that he said in his mini-sermon in Acts, chapter five, the crowd had a similar reaction: "After they heard this, they were cut to the heart..." However, these folks in chapter two, then asked, "what shall we do?" They didn't get mad at Peter. They went to a level of repentance! In this case, however, those who are cut to the heart had another reaction. They were unwilling to change, so they went into attack mode. When you are made to see yourself for who you are, you have two choices: You can seek change, or you can simply get mad start attacking as a way to cover up your need for change, and as a way to eliminate something that has made you uncomfortable—shown you that you need to change—that you are wrong. Those who may see the need for change and simply refuse to change must resort to attacking those who have made them see the need for change. For the authorities, it was easier for them to attack than to change. Again, this is true in everyday life. We encounter people all the time who become upset with us and exhibit rude, difficult behavior. In doing this, they make the situation worse for themselves, knowing that everyone can see their weaknesses. In those cases, it is not uncommon for people to get worse in their behavior, and this is what happened in Peter's day.

The authorities did finally determine that these brothers had to die. This is the same thing that was decided about Jesus. When they couldn't do anything else about Jesus, they concluded that they had to kill Him, and it is clear, in the text, that those who follow Jesus have to face what He faced. And, again, present day, when I examine my own life, there is no use in me claiming to be one of His followers if I'm not willing to put up with what He had to deal with. For the servant is not better than the master, and if the master must suffer so must those who follow him. You can't follow Jesus to the throne without a willingness to deal with the cross. You can't expect to have Sunday morning victory without Friday afternoon pain. Quit talking about favor, blessing and prosperity, if you aren't willing to talk about denying yourself, taking up your cross and following Him. To be a follower of Christ is to face what He faced. And, when you do reach your pinnacle and have done your time—gone through your own suffering—do not begrudge others their struggle or their success. Remember that we should all be trying to be more like Jesus and follow Him inherently. What you learn in your journey, you can share with others through behaviors and tolerance and acceptance of all that is yours—the struggles, the successes, and the people you encounter on both sides every day.

A SOLID PURPOSE: DOING THE WORK OF JESUS

The enemy had a plan. The enemy had intention. The intent was to destroy the people of God. Right about the time you read of the intention of the enemy, you also see the INTERRUPTION OF THE ALLY. When the enemy rises, so does the ally. "When they heard this, they were cut to the heart and wanted to put them to death. But a Pharisee intervened…" God interrupts the plan of the enemy. God has another plan. It's not time for the apostles to see death, so God interrupts their plan with His plan, because He still has purpose for them. And, it appears that God intervenes with an ally right on time. Sometimes we forget that God knows when to intervene; He knows when to step in. In this case, God interrupts the enemy's plan with His own plan. God intercepts the plan of the enemy. Who knows what could have happened to you, if the Lord had not interrupted the plan of the enemy right on time? Who knows where you would have been, had not the Lord intervened right on time? And this applies to any time in your life—in any situation. We must remember to support Jesus and His cause, and God will reward and intervene when He sees the need. Our purpose is solid and necessary when we do the work of Jesus in His name.

Our purpose is solid and necessary when we do the work of Jesus in His name.

And how can we do the work of Jesus. How, in our scripture here, was the work done? Simply by supporting Jesus and sticking by Him were these men spared death. In our own lives, do we feel that we could be spared further financial despair or heightened personal gain if we are faithful and actually apply that faith to doing God's work? Can we do something in our community? Have we given to the food back? Did we take care of our family? Did we go the extra mile for a friend? And, it's not like we have to do this everyday. Certainly, a good deed now and then is possible. And, certainly, as a result of that, habits will form; habits that will allow us to stay close to God and to advocate for God in any situation. Success is close. Who can we trust? Who can we reach out to? Chapters one and two taught us how to handle all that—now, one step further—can we accept or find our ultimate partners in faith. Will God spare us or advance us simply by what we do? Yes. And, can we find help and allies in unexpected places and in unexpected situations? Yes. Does all of this make it possible for outreach and habits that lead us to other pathways to God? Yes. All this leads to our solid purpose as Christians.

All this leads to our solid purpose as Christians.

Notice the identification of the ally. "They wanted to kill them, but a Pharisee..." The scene changes because of a Pharisee. The text does not read "but a fellow disciple...." "But a Pharisee..." This is not an ally you would expect. His name is Gamaliel. He is a Pharisee, which means he is on the side of the enemy. Someone from the side of enemy rises in behalf of God's people. He is a Pharisee, who has much influence. He is a member of the Sanhedrin. Moreover, in this case, he was the President of the Sanhedrin court during the reigns of Tiberius, Caligula, and Claudius. He was only one of seven Jewish scholars who were honored by the title "Rabban." Gamaliel was honored by the all the people. The Talmud said of him: "Since Rabban Gamaliel died, the glory of the Law has ceased." All of this is to say that although he is the enemy, he was the right enemy to have on their side. He was the enemy who had some influence. God raised the right one to speak in behalf of the apostles. On one hand, he is the enemy in this case; on the other hand, he happens to be the right enemy. God knows how to raise the right people to your side. There are times when Disciples of Christ can benefit from people of influence being on their side, even if those folks may not be disciples themselves. God raises up the right people at the right time. We, as His followers, need to remain open and aware of this.

Notice the communication of this ally, and, at the same time, remember that our allies may come in all forms. This unexpected ally is used to bring some level of calm. Gamaliel stands up and tells his comrades to think for a moment. He tells them to calm down based on a couple of historical examples. He asks them to recall Theudas and Judas, both historical figures who had taken bands of people and led revolts. He uses that example to calm the crowd and back the apostles, saying, "Just leave these men alone." Leave this movement alone. He goes on to say, "If this is of human origin it will fail; if it is of God, it will succeed." It is hard to judge Gamaliel here, because he does spare our heroes, but... we do need to examine the form in which this intervention came. And, we need to remain cognizant of the fact that these interventions may come in all forms and in all manners. We may not agree with our unexpected allies in life, but we can respect the fact that is it the Hand of God, and it is intended for a reason.

Regarding the text again: Gamaliel's advice was faulty on three fronts. First of all, he compares the movements of these other two troublemakers with that of the movement of Christ. Of course, there is a big difference between what those other two started, and what Jesus started. Theudas and Judas are not Jesus; therefore, while their revolt fizzled out, the one

Jesus started did not. We need to remember, present day, in any trouble that may come our way, Jesus was not simply some troublemaker who would fade off the scene; Jesus revolted for the truth.

MISTAKES AND HOW TO CLEARLY DEFINE OUR PATHWAY TO GOD

The second mistake Gamaliel made was that he told them to leave the movement alone. He told them to just remain neutral to this "Jesus thing". And, how often do we hear this in daily life? Do our co-workers and neighbors always understand our devotion to Jesus? No, but it shouldn't matter. We can't remain neutral to the cause of Christ. To remain neutral is to reject Christ. "Behold he stands at the door and knocks, if anyone hears his voice, let them open the door..." You can't remain neutral to Christ. When it comes to Christ there are no "undecided voters." You can remain neutral to political candidates, but you can't remain neutral to Christ. He stands here and you must make decision about Him! "Choose you this day whom you will serve."

The third mistake he makes is that he says that the success of this movement will determine whether or not it is of God. Gamaliel should know that there are some things that are not of God, which appear to be successful for a while. And there are some things, which are of God that are not always successful in human eyes, as we discussed at the beginning of this chapter. Gamaliel was a worldly pragmatist who was looking at this situation the wrong way. That notwithstanding, we should all applaud him for the last thing he says, "But if it is from God, you will not be able to stop these men; you will only find yourselves fighting against God." Even Gamaliel had sense enough to know that their arms were too short to box with God! Gamaliel may have already been sensing that they were in a no-win situation. He had seen how God freed these apostles. He had seen how the movement was unstoppably pressing on. Perhaps he sensed that they weren't just fighting against Peter and John; he sensed that somebody had their backs. Perhaps he sensed that they were fighting a losing battle! And this very thing we need to remember as we make our way through our daily lives. We learned in previous chapters to trust God and to preach His name. We learn here to allow it to guide us to success and enlightenment.

Whatever the case here, God uses this flawed logic for the sake of his people. This interruption by Gamaliel leads to the EMANCIPATION OF THE DISCIPLES. It was flawed, but it worked. He was the enemy, but it worked. God can even use the flawed things and people to bless you. And, this, again, we need to remain open to. Our allies may not be of our religion or our race or our gender, but they may present themselves regardless. We have to open, trusting, bold, and ready to accept God's Hand. Regarding the text, we know: "His speech persuaded them…", and, as a result, they were let go. This man was not the right one, and he didn't really say the right thing, but it worked anyway. It worked because God was in it. Right here when they needed it most, God used an unexpected ally to aid His children. God can do it. Sometimes God does use the enemy to aid you. Sometimes God does use people you would never expect to lift you up. God is so good, and God is so powerful, that God can use the unexpected ally to stand with you and for you.

The court is persuaded by Gamaliel's speech. They call the apostles to them, and they let them go. However, before they let them go, they whip them, and they flog them. The Jewish flogging consisted of 39 lashes. They stripped the shirts off of the accused criminals and used a whip made of calfskin to whip them across the back and the chest. In some cases, people would die from these lashes. These lashes left some scars on the apostles, but they made it out. They went through some suffering, but they made it out. Some of us here have some scars from what we've been through, but... we made it out. Some of us bear the proof of what you been through, but, because God stepped in, we made it out. And, not only did these men make it out with their scars, but they came out rejoicing. I wonder—can you rejoice with your scars? Can you rejoice with your wounds? Can you lift up holy hands with your wounds? Can you shout with your scars? Can you move forward in faith—in success—with the mistakes you've made? You have to. Learning and growing is all part of your faithful journey with God.

Take with you this fact: All of this happened because God blessed them with an unexpected ally. God blessed them with someone who was not like them. All of us have been blessed with an unexpected ally. When the enemy was ready to destroy us—when the sin and death hovered over us—when justice was ready strike us down—when we were all worthy of the capital punishment, one stood up for us and one will again. One spoke for us. Remember—this one may not be like us, but he helped us succeed. The message, readers, is clear—open up and see what is here for you in faith and in life. God sends us unexpected allies and opportunities. He tests our ability to open our hearts and minds—to trust and to test our faith against others. Only when we stand strong and accept even that which can make us uncomfortable or cause us to step out of our regular routine will we be rewarded by God.

CASE STUDY 1

TOLERANCE, TRUST, AND FINDING COMMON GROUND

We've discussed a number of concepts, thus far, in our quest to better our lives through our faith in God and our involvement with our communities, using that faith and trust in Him. We've established that it is often difficult to unconditionally trust anyone, and it is hard to go into situations that seem unfamiliar or unusual to us. Many times, this lack of trust in God, in the situation, even in ourselves, can lead to intolerance and a breakdown in communication and interaction with others in our community.

Earlier, I told a story from my travels about a multi-denominational park where different religions convene harmoniously and tolerance and respect for one another are the norm. In this place where places of worship and the people who frequent these places all have equal billing, the level of tolerance is a beautiful thing. To balance our tolerance for others with our pride in our own religion and our love of Jesus is another delicate issue.

As I reflect on all of this, I can recall a couple of different situations in which I observed trust, tolerance and the establishment of a common ground against a number of odds. The first is a story of worlds colliding - a case study in making friends and accepting another despite differences.

I met a woman on a business trip one time. As we sat, trying to kill time in the airport, trading stories about our families, our professions, and our experiences, she told me a story I'll never forget. Raised a Roman Catholic, she became involved with a mission project that was delivering meals to people whose homes were ravaged by Hurricane Katrina. Rushed and hurried one day, she struggled to throw together a quick side dish to go with the beautiful casseroles she had been working on all day from the comfort of her warm and safe kitchen. She settled on deviled eggs—a little mustard, a little mayo, some paprika—all on a throwaway plate. She drove, still hurried, thinking of her preschool pick up later—thankfully, in an area of Louisiana not ravaged by the hurricane—and her hair appointment the next day and how that would fit in with all her cooking. She drove past water-ravaged streets and homes literally washed away by the raging waters of the storm. Breathing a sigh of relief, she pulled into a neighborhood, her assigned area, which didn't seem too bad. She got out of her car, carefully pulled the hot casseroles from the back of her car and tried to look past the people hauling water-soaked carpets out of houses—ruined photos albums—dirty stuffed animals and broken furniture. Suddenly, she heard a tearful voice behind her. "Oh—you brought deviled eggs! I love deviled eggs. My mother used to make them all the time. She'd take them to church..." The voice trailed off.

Turning, she encountered a young woman, holding a little boy's hand. The woman was crying big tears and shaking her head. "I'm sorry," she said, "But we lost my mom in the storm. We lost our church too." Stunned at her candor, the woman pulled back a little, unable to speak. She told me that at that moment—watching this lovely young woman, standing in all this ruin, holding her precious boy's hand—that she suddenly felt the gravity of what she was doing—providing comfort and familiarity to people who had lost everything. While she had quickly thrown together a side dish with little thought, wrapped up in her own religious, familial, and personal needs, she had not once thought that a simple meal—a simple memory—connection with another of a different religion, from a different neighborhood—would ever mean so much. And, yet, it did. And, she knew, that one day, it would come full circle and she would be grateful for a home cooked meal—a sympathetic ear—a friendly face or even just the attention of someone who cared—not just for that five minute encounter but for the rest of his or her life. Suddenly, connection meant something to her for the first time—in that simple moment—with her simple food offering.

I also have the opportunity to interact with young people in my ministry. And, in this last brief case study, if you will, I want to point out a daily observation of mine. At school, I hear all the time how the pretty, popular people are treated one way while the shyer, more reserved academics are treated another—how the theater, music, and dance people hang out together—or how the athletes keep to themselves. The lists and stereotypes go on and on. Often, I worry that, in these situations, our young people are building intolerances and creating lifestyles that will leave them insensitive to others and their needs. Yet, when I observe them in worship—or when I see that, without the barriers that exist in school—without those preconceived notions of one another –they do interact without issues. They sit, worshipful, sharing common ground in their love of God, their security in being part of a community, and their closeness to their families. In this common area, without prejudice or expectation—aside from loving God and others—they share stories, they support one another, and they build lifelong relationships that will serve them well later in life. Maybe they don't have the same interests, the same family background, or the same talents, but they do share in their love of God and their involvement in their church communities.

4

BEYOND THE COMFORT ZONE

STEPPING OUTSIDE THE NORM FOR AN ELEVATED LIFE EXPERIENCE

ADJUSTING TO THE TIMES: WHAT WE CAN LEARN FROM THE ISLEY BROTHERS AND OTHER FAVORITE ARTISTS

There aren't many musical artists that have hit singles in six different decades. Most artists are "one hit wonders." Nowadays, an artist will have one hit, and the public doesn't hear from him/her anymore. That wasn't the case with the group that started off as a gospel quartet and included, the then unknown men: Kelly, Rudy, Ronnie, and Vernon Isley. This group of men is better known as the now forever popular Isley Brothers. The Isley brothers are one of the only groups to have had hit singles in six different decades. In the late 1950's, it was the single "Shout"; in the 60's it was songs like "It's Your Thing..."; in the 70's there were protest songs like "Fight the Power" and ballads like "For the Love of You"; into the 80's there was "Don't Say Goodnight"; the 90's brought us collaborations with R. Kelly like "Down Low"; in 2001 there was "Contagious"; and the list goes on and on (Recording group / artist, 1954—present: Motown,

T-Neck, Warner Brothers, Def Soul Labels). One of the reasons that the group, the Isley Brothers, was successful for so long was their willingness to adjust to the times by changing their sound and their lyrics. They refused to be stuck in various musical traditions of certain periods. Although they maintained the core of their identity, they knew how to make certain tweaks in order to stay relevant. They grew and prospered, because they "pushed the envelope" and were willing to venture beyond the musical comfort zone. This is not always an easy thing to achieve.

OUR SCRIPTURE REFERENCE: DID THE EARLY CHURCH PUSH BEYOND THE COMFORT ZONE?

Regarding the church, segments of the early organization were also willing to push beyond the comfort zone. At first glance, this passage—Acts 11:19-21—seems to simply be a tangential, succinct progress report on the early church. It's easy to overlook the text here as just a bit of irrelevant information. But, something is happening here. A corner is turned in this text. There is a quiet revolution articulated in these few verses. There is a radical shift happening here. The movement of God is occurring in an unprecedented way. This text is central in salvation history. One reference book lists the seventy most important events in the Bible, and along with events like "Creation", "the flood", "the crucifixion, and "the resurrection", this event is included. The establishment of the church in Antioch is included as one of the 70 most important events in the Bible. So—what is exactly happening here that is so relevant to our modern lives?

Something was happening. Philipp had had the nerve to go to despised Samaria and preach the Gospel. He made his way to Gaza, and on the way ran into an Ethiopian official, a man who happened to have been reading from Isaiah. Philipp asks the man if he understands what he is reading. The Ethiopian basically says, "I need someone to explain it to me." Philipp does just that; explains it to him, and the Ethiopian receives the Word and is, then, baptized. As I said, something is happening. There are change and movement. Later, the Lord deals with Peter and an Italian military leader named Cornelius simultaneously in different places. In one instance, He shows Cornelius, in a vision, that he is supposed to send after Peter and to hear his word. And, He shows Peter a vision in which he convinces him that nothing made by God can be called unclean, setting him up for his eventual interactions. Eventually, Peter is escorted to the home of Cornelius, where he also declares the word of God. Cornelius and his people accept the word, receive the Spirit and are, likewise, baptized. Now this "something" is expanding.

Do we notice change and movement in our own worlds? Do we pay attention to the church changing and growing? Do we stop to think about how our family and friends are changing and evolving—how our relationships with them are moving and becoming dynamically different? It is hard to step out of our own comfort zones regarding even noticing change sometimes—let alone, try to facilitate change. And yet, this is sometimes what God asks us to do. And, many times, He works in those often alluded to "mysterious ways". We don't always notice or see what He is doing right away; the desired outcome becomes more apparent after the fact. If we keep our eyes open enough in these cases, we can become experts or at least somewhat proficient in noticing what we need to notice—when we need to step in for someone, facilitate change at work or in church—advocate for God or Jesus in some way.

WHAT IS REALLY HAPPENING IN OUR SCRIPTURE VERSE HERE?

So, again, something is happening. God is "sneaking" the church into the lives of people otherwise untouched by it. God is moving the church in another direction. In a very subtle way, the make up of the church is changing. The church in these Acts is no longer the "good old boys club." However, not everyone in the church is happy regarding where God is taking it. The church is becoming more diversified, and it is a painful transition. Some of the folks in Acts want their old church back. It is interesting to note when people want something back, which they think was theirs—and, all along, it was given to them to begin with. Even today, we forget that we became members of a church, and others are worthy of the same, but allowing people unlike us or raised with different beliefs in is sometimes difficult. There are some folks who take ownership of the church as if they founded it, died for it, rose for it, and are coming back for it. I am always intrigued when certain sectors of American society have these flag-waving rallies in which they talk about wanting their country back. They want it back from "whom?" It was never theirs. The only folks who can rightfully say that they want their country back are the Native Americans! Sometimes, we all forget what is really "ours" and what is something that should belong to everyone.

Sometimes, we all forget what is really "ours" and what is something that should belong to everyone.

WHEN GOD'S MOVEMENT ISN'T ALWAYS OBVIOUS TO US, SOMETIMES WE HAVE TO STEP OUT OF OUR COMFORT ZONES

Again, something is happening in the book of Acts. God is doing "something!" The movement of God is not always obvious; sometimes it works on its own, doing its thing, under the radar. Without it, without movement and change, nothing works! Yet, we don't always feel or see the change. When you bake in the kitchen, get all your recipes out and prepare for a family meal, do you think about what you're not doing to make it all work? Do you think about the things you set in motion without thought that may bring about a positive result? Picture that baking time with the family. You mix up the dough, like you always do, maybe throw in some salt, sugar, baking powder, and yeast—like you always do—never questioning what will happen. And... that yeast creates the bread, makes it rise and change so that the family can enjoy it, partake of it. Picture that yeast, which spreads slowly but surely through the dough. Or your herb garden: You tend it, water it, plant it, etc. Do you think about the seeds and what your movement—your action —does to change them? Movement and change are like the tiniest mustard seeds, which grow into a bush. God is pushing the church beyond a comfort zone and, thankfully, some folks in this early church begin to catch on.

And, we did talk about this earlier—this way that God sometimes works. Often, His goals and His lessons for us are not obvious. It takes that learned recognition that we touched on previously. Just as we know our way around the kitchen for a certain recipe so, too, must we learn our way around what God expects from us and when to change it up a bit—for that positive change and movement from our comfort zone that we've been discussing.

WHAT DOES THIS SCRIPTURE VERSE SAY ABOUT MAINTAINING OUR IDENTITIES IN GOD?

This brief narrative, however, says that there were those who were yet ATTACHED TO TRADITION. Verse 19 starts off very well. There were those who had been scattered by the persecution of Stephen, who traveled as far as Phoenicia, Cyprus and Antioch. When they were scattered, they spread the Word. Wherever they went, they took the Word with them. They did not stop being who they were just because they ran into some trouble. They maintained their identity in the midst of adversity. They were preaching Jesus before their problems; they kept preaching Jesus in the midst of their problems. They worshiped before their trouble, now they worshiped in their trouble. They did not allow what they were going through to strip them of their ministry and identity. As a matter of fact, their trouble served to further the cause of Christ. The enemy did not know what he was scattering when he scattered them. He was scattering seed. When you scatter seed, it just might grow and prosper into wherever it is meant to be. We applaud this crowd for being productive no matter where they were. There was a farmer who painted John 3:16 on his weather vane. A curious neighbor asked him, "What are you trying to say by painting that on your weather?" "Are you trying to say that God's word is as unstable as the wind? "No," replied the farmer, "I'm trying to say that no matter which way the wind blows, the gospel is still true." That's what these scattered saints believed.

Hence, we applaud them for their activity. At the same time, I have some issues with their ministry. The narrator reports that "those who had been scattered...traveled as far as...spreading the word ONLY among the Jews." The writer emphasizes the word "only." It is as though he knows that something is not right about this. There is a move of God in chapters 8-11, but not everyone is connected to that move. The writer accentuates the fact that there are those who are yet holding on to what use to be. Spreading the Gospel to the Jews only is what had been going on for a while. For this crowd, "tradition" had become traditionalism. Tradition in itself is good. It comes from the word "tradition" which means bridge. Tradition is that bridge which has gotten us over. I praise God for some of the bridges, which have gotten us over in our churches. Those traditions should not necessarily be discarded. I am thankful for the richness of the hymns; I am thankful for the preaching styles of yesteryear, which were so creative and rhythmic. I am thankful for the praying missionary sisters wearing their white whose prayers brought us over. We need the traditions; we just need to keep growing, moving, and learning—changing into what we are meant to be—what was set on course with those traditions long ago.

However, there is a danger when tradition becomes traditionalism. "Traditionalism" is the worship of tradition. Traditionalism is to make tradition an idol god. Traditionalism is to make tradition an absolute. One man has said that "tradition" is the living faith of the dead, and traditionalism is the dead faith of the living. Traditionalism supposes that nothing should be done the first time. Only what has been done should be done. Some of the Scribes and Pharisees had problems with Jesus, because He came breaking their traditions. They put Him on a cross, because they could not handle their sacred traditions being broken. "....spreading the word only among the Jews...." They didn't sense the move of God, or if they sensed it, they resisted it. It would not have been surprising if they resisted it because change is difficult. And, for many of us modern day, we are taught that tradition is good and change is to be regarded with caution. We have to learn to discern between good and change and ineffective change. We also have to pay attention to when tradition can become cumbersome and, in a way, disallow us to move beyond our safe zones—our comfort zones. Of course, as we are discussing at length in this chapter, it is imperative to allow movement and change when appropriate.

WHEN, READERS, CAN TRADITION BE RESTRICTIVE?

Tradition can be so ingrained that you don't even question it, even if it does not make sense. You won't question it even if it is hindering the growth of the kingdom of God. Some traditions need to be questioned, but we can so duped by tradition that we can't even step out of it. Some of the things we do in our churches need to be questioned. Some of our traditional modes of worship, administration, church meetings, and outreach need to come under question. We have "stuff "and do "stuff" and have no idea why! The problem is that we can get so stuck to where we are and who we are that we desire nothing different, even if it will be an upgrade. We want sameness, even if it halts progress. Two caterpillars were crawling across the grass when a butterfly flew over them. They looked up, and one nudged the other and said, "You couldn't get me up in one of those things for a million dollars." And, as humans, we do this too—fail to see our potential or the path on which we are supposed to travel. Tradition provides security. It is unnerving to do things a different way. It is unnerving to move beyond the comfort zone. Changes in worship are unnerving. Changes in by-laws are unnerving. It would have been unnerving to take the Gospel outside of the Jews.

Tradition provides security.

"Now those who had been scattered…traveled as far as…spreading the Word only among Jews." The reason it was so easy for them to maintain their tradition was because they believed God sanctioned what they were doing. They did not hear the original marching orders. "But you shall receive power…and you will be my witnesses in Jerusalem; Judea, Samaria, and to the ends of the earth…" They only heard half of what the Lord says. It's easy to co-opt God to your side when you've only heard half of what He has said. It's easy to focus on a part of the counsel of God to support your cause instead of hearing the whole counsel of God. It is so easy to attach God to a cause. Slave-owners attached God to their cause; European Settlers attached God to the cause of conquering American frontiers; supporters of Apartheid in South Africa attached God to their cause; Nazis in Germany attached God to their cause; Israelis attach God to their cause as well as Palestinians. Conservatives do! Liberals do! We use God for our own agendas.

These folks who only went to the Jews believed that God was on their side. People get sensitive when they feel like their traditions are backed and justified by God. We get our own prejudices mixed up with the will of God. We get our own upbringings mixed up with the Word of God. God bless grandma, but her word might not be equivalent with God's Word. Some folks won't move out of certain seats, because they believe God wants them there. And, just as we said earlier, sometimes movement from that seat—away from that tried and true recipe—towards that new way of thinking—is necessary.

BECOMING "AWARE OF THE MOMENT" IN ORDER TO STEP OUT OF THAT RESTRICTIVE COMFORT ZONE!

There are those in this text who seem to be attached to tradition. But, there are also those here who seem to be AWARE OF THE MOMENT. While many of them were attached to tradition, some of them were aware of the moment. Many of them who had been scattered spread the Word to the Jews only. However, some of them take the Word to some Hellenistic gentiles. The phrase "some of them" implies that it wasn't many of them. "Some of them" implies that it wasn't the majority. The "some of them" could not wait for the rest of them to get on board. If "some of them" waited on the rest of them, then this move may have never taken place. Later on, after much "back and forth", the rest of them catch up to the "some of them." The "some of them" crowd hopes and prays that the rest of them catch up, but you can't wait for that. Every movement, every new initiative in a church; every building program; every new initiative in a community requires a "some of them." Progress and innovation do not stand on the shoulders of the "rest of them"; it stands on the shoulders of some of them. The "some of them" cannot be deterred or discouraged because of the lack cooperation of the rest of them. You have to go forward as God has revealed, not in arrogance but in humble obedience. Every church needs a "some of them" crowd. Every trustee ministry, every choir, every youth ministry, every men's ministry, every diaconate ministry needs a few folks in them who are a part of the "some of them" crowd. "Some of them" crowds have changed the course of history, and that is good!

So, are we intrigued by this "some of them" crowd? Do we want to be liked by this crowd? Do we seek their approval or do we eschew what they do because it doesn't fit our comfort zone or out traditions? Do we then do what countless people before us have and begin to criticize them or move away from the positive change they may influence? We need to resist this. And, I say this because, sometimes, we don't realize we do it. And what do these "some people" do, really?

"Some of them" pushed beyond the comfort zone. They pushed beyond the comfort zone by spreading the Gospel in Antioch. Antioch was a great city. A half-million people lived there during these times. It was the third largest city in the known world behind Rome and Alexandria. The main street was four miles long and was paved with marble. This street was lined on both sides with marble colonnades. It was the only ancient city which had streets lighted at night. It was some kind of a city—yet these scattered saints were not intimidated by all that Antioch had to offer. They recognize that the one thing this city did not have was the Gospel. And no matter what else it had to offer, what they had to offer was essential. So they preached there anyway!

WHAT DOES THIS BIBLICAL REFERENCE MEAN TO US, MODERN DAY?

In addition to that, Antioch was the Las Vegas of the ancient world. It was the gambling capital. Chariot races were popular in Antioch, and the betting on these races was even more popular than the races themselves. Yet, these scattered saints were not so involved in what was going on in Antioch that they forgot about their purpose, and that was to get the word out! It is possible to be so involved in the world that we forget about our responsibility to the world to be the salt of the earth? They were not intimidated by the grandeur; they weren't too involved in the activity, and they weren't so turned off by the immorality. There were some wild things going on in Antioch. A few miles outside the city of Antioch, there was a shrine dedicated to Daphne, a Greek goddess said to have had love affair with one of the Greek gods. The temple was staffed by prostitutes who performed sexual acts with the worshippers as rituals, which helped them to identify with Daphne herself. These kinds of things made Antioch a dark place. Nevertheless, the saints weren't so saintly that they could not make contact with this dark city. Christians have to do more than "shaking their heads" at the condition of society. We have to go into change mode. Contact is necessary even if it means risking contamination. The Gospel to the broader world got its start in a dark city like Antioch. That's where the Gospel is at it's best. The brightness of the glorious Gospel shines most conspicuously in the dark corners of society.

These scattered saints push beyond the comfort zone by spreading the Gospel to some non-Jews. This was historic. This was revolutionary. This was earth shattering. No one else was really doing this. A couple of the church leaders like Peter and Philipp had made contact with the Gentiles. But, these were unnamed persons. These were ordinary folks. You don't have to be "important" to do something important. You don't have to be a big shot to do something big. They break with the customary. They do the unusual. It was not comfortable. It was scary. But that's what they did. They recognize that real ministry means going beyond the comfort zone. It may mean doing what no one else is doing. It may mean doing what we've been doing in a different way. It means having a Star Trek mentality: "boldly going where no one has gone before." It may mean taking the "road less traveled." It means getting dirty. It means operating outside of your personal comfort level.

How many of us can say that we have traveled somewhere unknown, looked past what was going on, and let our beliefs and our morals guide others? On a daily basis, how many times do we have this opportunity? To guide a friend off the wrong path? To help a teenager? To hold back judgment on the person asking for money on the street? Or, further, to rise above the others in the workplace when we know someone is being wronged? To stop something from happening in a social situation when we know someone is being hurt? Despite tradition and the mentality that "this is how it always is"?

READER'S PAUSE

LIVING WELL: HOW TO MOVE BEYOND YOUR COMFORT ZONE

In the next chapter, we discuss how we might take our faith with us. To do that, we have to move out of our comfort zones. Detail here a time when you did that for God, for your family, or to stand up to another. Be specific.

AND WHAT DOES OUR SCRIPTURE SAY AGAIN?

I wonder what it was that pushed them to do it. Peter only went to Cornelius because the Lord showed him a vision. Philipp only went to the Ethiopian because the Spirit spoke directly to him. What pushed these ordinary folks? There is no indication that they were aware of the activity of Peter, which would have provided incentive for them to preach to non-Jews. Aside from them just sensing the move of God, the clue might be in where they were from. Luke does not waste words. These men and women were from Cyprus and Cyrene. Both Cyprus and Cyrene were places that were not a part of the mainstream of society. Cyrene was an African city from which Simon had come. Simon was the one who was made to bear the cross for Jesus. Tradition has it that this same Simon who was made to bear the cross, to the Gospel back to his homeland. That day changed his life. Simon was racially profiled and made to carry the cross. It is believed that Simon passed this Gospel down to his children, and it went on from there. The people from Cyrene were used to being outsiders. They were once on the fringes. They were once aliens to the commonwealth of Israel. Recognition of their own past made them more sensitive to the need to get the Word to other outsiders!

The truth is there was a time when many of us were not where we are right now. Recognition of your own past should motivate you to push beyond the comfort zone. Recognition of your own past should make you sympathetic to folks who don't know the Lord yet. You weren't always saved! You were once in the streets, you used to hustle, or you were languishing in depression. Maybe there was a time when even you had everything but still felt empty. Consciousness of their own past may have motivated these scattered saints to have a sense of the moment.

These scattered saints who push beyond the comfort zone end up experiencing the APPROVAL OF GOD. These ordinary folks go to this intimidating, immoral city and end up having success in ministry: "a great number of people believed and turned to the Lord." How do you explain that? These weren't professional preachers. They had not studied at the feet of Gameiel.

There's only one explanation: "the Lord's hand was with them…" They had help from heaven. The favor of God rested on them. When the Lord's hand is with you, you can do what people think can't be done! When the Lord's hand is with you, you can accomplish what your family members said couldn't happen. When the Lord's hand is with a church, they can achieve goals, which seemed impossible. There were many folks who were not with them in this endeavor to get the word to Gentiles. But, they did have one ally who mattered, and that was Jehovah. And if God is there for you, it does not matter who is against you.

It's not as though the presence of the Lord caught up with them. It 's not as though they pushed beyond the comfort zone, and God accompanied them. God's hand was already there; they just caught up with God. If we want to experience the favor of God, we have to catch up with God. God is already active beyond the comfort zone. A church, which is stuck in traditionalism, misses out on the manifested presence of God. God already is where he is beckoning us to come! Maybe the church needs to catch up with God.

5

DON'T LEAVE HOME WITHOUT IT!

TAKING YOUR FAITH WITH YOU

OUR SCRIPTURE REFERENCE: THE DAY THEY ARRESTED JESUS

In Acts 1:4–5, they thought it was all over. They had assumed that this chapter in their lives was over. They were in the garden with Jesus when Judas and the authorities came to arrest Him. The disciples saw the kiss of the betrayer. They watched as impetuous Peter brandished his sword, cut off the soldier's ear, and, then, how Jesus healed this soldier who was His enemy. These same disciples observed, with broken hearts, as their Lord and our Lord was led away by this arresting mob. Most of them fled after that. A couple of them stayed in the vicinity and saw how Jesus was lead from kangaroo court to kangaroo court. Peter was close by but not too close. He was close enough to be identified with this madman, as some thought, claiming to be the Messiah. Yet, he was far enough away in spirit to deny his relationship with Jesus three times. After that, even Peter deserted Jesus as he escaped into the darkness of his own sorrow and shame.

DID THE STORY END WITH THE CRUCIFIXION?

They heard the report of how Jesus was crucified. He wasn't alone. There were two other criminals crucified with Him. There were three crucified that Friday. One died from sin—one died in sin—but that one in the middle, Jesus, died for sin. These disciples weren't there, but they heard the rumor that as He was dying there was a seismic shifting of the earth, which resulted in an earthquake and that there was a midnight, mid-day eclipse. Word came to them that Joseph of Arimithaea requested the body of Jesus. And so he buried Him in a tomb, which he had secured. Jesus had not secured His own burial place. There was no need for Him to make that investment, because, as we all know, He only needed a tomb on temporary terms.

Having heard this, the disciples indeed thought the story was over. But then something strange happened. Early in the morning on the first day of the week, some women came running to them, telling them that He was risen. The grave was empty. The sealed stone had been rolled away. Sitting on that stone was a messenger informing them that He was not there, but that He was risen. The disciples had a hard time believing the sisters until Jesus appeared unto them Himself. He showed them the nail-prints in His hands and feet, and they were shocked and confused, as we all would be.

These disciples were stranded at the intersection of belief and disbelief. Therefore, as this first chapter of Acts declares, Jesus appeared to them for a period of forty days. He kept appearing to them giving them "convincing" or "infallible" proofs. I'm not sure exactly what these proofs were, but whatever they were, they were proofs, which could not be denied. The fact that Jesus had to keep appearing to them with these convincing proofs means that they still weren't convinced. Jesus keeps showing up, because these disciples needed to believe. There would be no ministry if they did not believe. They couldn't preach what they weren't convinced of. So Jesus keeps showing up. He will show up as much as necessary. Jesus does not frown on doubt, but he does seek to transform the doubters. As you are wallowing in your own disbelief and disillusionment, He will show up. Around you, He will supply convincing proofs of what He is able to do. When you are having a hard time believing, the Lord will supply what's necessary for you to believe. Sometimes you have to have the right kind of eye to see these convincing proofs. But, He will supply what is necessary. The Lord will not give up on our obstinate, stubborn unbelief. He keeps showing up!

Jesus does not frown on doubt, but he does seek to transform the doubters.

A CRUCIAL CONVERSATION: WHEN TO PAUSE–WHEN TO STAY OPEN–AND WHEN TO KEEP YOUR FAITH WITH YOU

On one particular day, in the midst of these appearances, Jesus has a crucial conversation with these disciples. In this conversation, He challenges them to take a SIGNIFICANT PAUSE. He says, "Do not leave Jerusalem, but to, instead, wait ..." This occurred while He was eating with them. On one hand, the fact that He was eating with them is strange. It is strange, because Jesus did not need to eat. He was raised with His glorified body; hence, there was no need for Him to eat. But, the fact that He was eating with them could be another one of those convincing proofs. The rumor was going around that this so-called risen Jesus was nothing more than a disembodied spirit, and that His body was not actually resurrected. In case His own followers were struggling with this idea, He does some things to show that He had a physical body, and one of those things was to eat with them. The fact that Jesus was eating with them could simply be a way for Him to share in fellowship with them before He departed from their presence. There needed to be some intimate time between them, and dining together would bring them together. He wanted them to be comfortable in His presence, and, in this way, He helped them to understand what was transpiring. And, as I mentioned before, we all have to stay open to what He may present us in our own lives. We have to keep our faith with us and remain open to what Jesus is trying to show us—as a path—as rejuvenation—as belief.

As Jesus eats with them, He tells them to stay in Jerusalem. By now, having been convinced of the Resurrection, the disciples were probably ready to get this news out. For them, the resurrection meant the beginning of a new era. God started something new in the resurrection. This was a new chapter for them. A new day had begun. They were anxious to get started with this new enterprise. They were like a horse, which couldn't wait to get out of the stall. There was a world waiting for them out there.

Before the disciples left, however, there was still something else they needed. No matter how anxious they were to start this new life, Jesus said, "Don't leave yet!" They had good training, for they had spent three years with Him. He had shown the disciples what ministry was like. They heard Him teach. These disciples had learned good doctrine. But, something was still missing. Even after the Lord had formed the first human being out of the dust of the earth, this man still wasn't alive until the Lord blew the breath of life into his nostrils. Even after the bones had come together; even after the muscle, tendons, flesh, and skin had come upon this bones, there still was no life in that open valley until Ezekiel called upon the Spirit to fill these new and improved bodies.

THE VIRTUE OF PATIENCE AND HOW IT AFFECTS OUR FAITH

In fact, Jesus often tells us that to get what we need to make it in life, we all need to wait. In order to live effectively, for Him, in the world, you need to wait. In order for all of us to change the world, we do need to wait. His message to us is that we should not be so anxious to get started that we leave home without what we need. Our blessing is in the waiting—when we gather the fortitude—when we reflect on what we believe—as we prepare for what is intended of us. Job said "all of my appointed time will I wait until my change comes." The psalmist says, "Wait on the Lord, be of good courage, and he shall strengthen thy heart." The prophet says, "They that wait on the Lord shall renew their strength…" There is something transformative in just waiting.

There is something transformative in just waiting.

READER'S PAUSE

LIVING WELL: HOW TO TAKE YOUR FAITH WITH YOU

We can't always preach the Word of God to people we don't know or where we think it might not be appropriate—at a dinner party, at work, or in other social situations. We can, however, live as examples to others and keep God foremost in our daily actions. Some people take mission trips—others take positions in the church—and still others simply make the Word of God clear in their homes. Recall a time or a moment here when you feel that you felt and reflected the Word of God. Maybe you gave food to your local Food Bank or money to a charity, but detail here when you felt that you were truly representing God and your faith—taking it with you.

____

____

____

____

____

Jesus is challenging the disciples to take what renowned Swiss Reformed theologian, Karl Barth, would call "a significant pause." Pause before you jump into the rat race. Between His resurrection and His ascension, Jesus was challenging them to pause. Between the ascension of Christ and the descending of the Spirit, these anxious disciples were being told to wait. How difficult it is to wait when you feel like you have what's necessary to get started!? How difficult it is to wait when you feel like you have what is necessary to be successful? But, if the Lord is putting you in a waiting position, you have to trust that there is something else He needs to do. God knows when you are ready for the next move before you know that you are ready. I have to learn how to trust what God is doing while I'm waiting. Waiting is not always wasted time; waiting is necessary time so that you don't waste time. They simply needed to trust the Lord on this one. And, we all have stories that test us in this way.

God knows when you are ready for the next move before you know that you are ready.

WHEN SHOULD WE KNOW WHEN TO TAKE OUR "SIGNIFICANT PAUSES" AND LIVE IN THE EXAMPLE OF THE DISCIPLES?

Recently, I was on a plane, ready to land. The pilot said that we were making a final descent into Newark airport. But, something happened; we started circling. And then, I knew we were in a holding pattern over Newark airport. I've done it so many times that I know when we are in that holding pattern. Of course, I got impatient—I started to sigh—even started complaining to the person next to me. Finally, the pilot spoke through the intercom and told us that one of the runways was being repaired; therefore, there was a back up. He said, "As soon as the other runway is clear, we can land." At that point, all I could do was just trust the one who was in charge! I couldn't see ahead of me. I could only see where I was. But, there was someone with better knowledge than I had who knew what was up ahead. If he says wait, I have to wait. And in these moments, we all need to remember that Jesus told the disciples to wait—to take a significant pause, because he knew what was up ahead. They could only see where they were, but the Lord could see where they were headed. And He knew what was necessary based on where they were going! Many times in life, we will feel impatient, we will question why certain things are happening to us in life, and we will lose focus or want to jump ship, so to speak. We need to remember these lessons in patience and waiting and, moreover, we need to note that, given the wait and the reflection, something better may be in store for us—or something bigger may be expected of us. Only the Lord knows, and we need to trust that and find serenity in that.

This waiting that we are told to do really will give us some form of serenity in some way. Even if we feel that we are up to the waiting, however, many times, we are not up to the task of determining when we have been asked to take our significant pause—to think of either the greater good or the repercussions of actions that are not thought through at all. Patience is a concept that we are taught and tested on from the time we are young, but are we ever really ready for selective determination or deciding when it is OK to be impatient and make things happen in that way—and when it is time to sit back and wait for the next significant signal or direction in our circumstances—in our lives?

WHEN WE'RE TOLD TO "WAIT"

"Do not leave Jerusalem but wait." This word wait literally means, "sit." In the words of Biblical Scholar, Frederick Dale Bruner, "sitting is not the position of heroes," nevertheless this is what Jesus told them to do! Jesus says I know you are anxious for the next move, but go somewhere and sit down. You think you are ready. But, you need to go somewhere and sit down. In this conversation, Jesus tells them to take this significant pause because of the SURE PROMISE. What are they waiting for? "Do not leave Jerusalem, but wait for the gift my Father promised, which you heard me speak about." Do not leave Jerusalem…" Something was going to happen in Jerusalem. Jerusalem was the epicenter of holy-history. It was right outside of Jerusalem where Jesus died. Calvary was connected to Jerusalem. Now this next event would happen in Jerusalem. For whatever reason, God had made Jerusalem the center of His activity.

Jesus tells them to wait on the gift, which the Father had promised. He tells them to wait because of a promise. There was no contract; it was just a promise. There had been no physical evidence of the truth of the promise, but they were to wait anyway, because it was the Father who had made the promise. Waiting makes sense when it is God who you are waiting for. It only makes sense to wait on the fulfillment of a promise when you can count on the one who has made the promise. Verbal promises are not too reliable in our world. During campaign seasons you here a myriad of promises coming from candidates. You wonder if all of them will be honored or if it's possible for some of them to be honored. You don't have to wonder about that with God. God is no politician. If God is the one who has done the promising, you can rest on it! You can go to sleep on nothing more than His promises. "Tis so sweet to trust in Jesus, just to take Him at His word. Just to rest upon His promise. Just to know it was said by God...Jesus, Jesus —how I trust Him...how I've proved Him more and more." Waiting makes sense when it's God you're waiting for. The disciples were being told to put their lives on hold. There are some things and some people for whom you might not want to put your life on hold, but God is worth putting things on hold. And, remember, better things may be in store for you—the wait may provide the rest and reflection you need—or you may be called upon in other capacities. It is always best to remember that God knows what will work for you, and only He can see what is in store for all of us.

Jesus says to wait, because God has promised you something. He says wait, because He has affirmed what God has promised. They have two reasons to take this significant pause. God said it. Jesus "amended it." Jesus is God's "amen" anyway. All of God's promises find their "amen" in Jesus. With this promise, we have double security. God said it and Jesus was over in the corner somewhere saying "amen." "Amen" means it is true. Jesus spoke about what God promised. The disciples could count on this promise, because they had double security. The promise that Jesus is referring to is the promise of the Holy Spirit. Over and again Jesus said someone is coming who would be present with him or her. He told them that another "comforter" was coming. He told them that it was necessary for Him to go away so that the Father could send another person to bring them spiritual guidance and reassurance in their respective roles in all this. And it was heavy stuff; their leader was gone, people were being arrested, and the idea existed that they all might be rebels or prophets. Jesus, in all this, had been their comforter. Suddenly, for the disciples, someone else is coming along—a new spiritual leader if you will. They are being asked to trust the Holy Spirit. For many of us—and even the disciples—the Holy Spirit is too abstract to consider, let alone trust and follow. The Holy Spirit is God incarnate—Jesus speaks through the Holy Spirit—the Holy Trinity becomes complete in our lives with the Holy Spirit and, yet, it can be hard to grasp.

Again, in the text, Jesus says that no matter whatever else the disciples have, they should not leave Jerusalem without His presence—just as He tells us in our daily lives to not leave our current situations without our faith and our direction from Him upon us or with us. In the text, the Lord knew what and whom the disciples were going to face, so He told them to wait until they got what they needed. When they entered the larger world, He knew that the disciples would be faced with the challenge of ministry, the opposition of the enemy, and the obstacles in trying to maintain their own integrity as his disciples. There was no way that they could do ministry, face the enemy, and maintain integrity without the power of the Holy Spirit. Here, we find that ministry is trying to change the world—that the enemy is dealing with difficult people—and that maintaining integrity is trying to be obedient in the face of temptation. Was this too much for them to do on their own? Is it too much for us now? The disciples needed help from on high! In other words, in order for them to be a fruitful church and live fruitful lives, they needed some invisible help. That help would be the Holy Ghost. This is the help that most of us need even today, and we need to remember that—again, to lead fruitful, successful, enlightened, and fulfilled lives.

Our situation really is both different from the disciples and also the same. It is different in that the Lord is not telling us to wait to be baptized with the Spirit in the same way they were to wait. The coming of the Spirit was a one-time event. This pouring out of the Spirit was to happen at one historical moment. That moment would occur on the day of Pentecost. The experience is not to be duplicated. That has happened. That's done. Although the Holy Spirit has been poured out on the church, you don't experience Him personally until you say yes to Christ as your Savior. The moment you say "yes" to Jesus Christ as Savior, the Spirit of God indwells you and rests upon you. After you receive Christ, you don't have to wait for the second blessing of the Spirit. You are baptized with the Spirit; you are clothed in the Spirit of God; the Spirit of God begins to live in you, the moment you say yes to the Lord. You are infused by the Spirit right now. You have been baptized with the Spirit. Use this baptism to take your message and your light into the world and to become the best person you can become.

It is often difficult to make and maintain contact with the Spirit in this hectic world. However, each day we do need to consciously attempt to come into contact with that Spirit who dwells in us and on us. Although we have the Spirit, I'm not sure that we know it. Waiting for us means sit still at home for minute and connect with the presence of God before you leave home. Don't leave home without a consciousness of His Spirit. Before you leave home, there are some things you make sure you have.

You make sure you have your keys. You make sure you have your wallet or purse. Or at least you have your money. And Lord knows you make sure you have your cell phone. We will turn around and go back and get that cell phone. We make sure we have all of our other gadgets. In addition to all of that, please make sure you leave with a consciousness that you dwell in the Spirit and that He dwells in you. Before you go to school, work, or wherever, make sure you leave with a consciousness of the Spirit. Quick aside: Young people many of you have gone back to school. Each morning, you ought to remind yourself that God lives in me! As you go back to school, go back with the knowledge that the Spirit of God lives in you.

It is often difficult to make and maintain contact with the Spirit in this hectic world.

We also are challenged with ministry, the enemy, and maintaining integrity. We can't change the world; we can't deal with the enemy; we can't deal with maintaining our integrity on our own. The Spirit will give us power to witness to the Gospel. The Spirit will give us power to deal with difficult people. The Spirit will give us power to live for the Lord in the face of temptation. We can't do it alone. Don't leave home without Him!

6

DIVINE DELIVERANCE

REVISITING THE STORY OF PETER: HAVE YOU EVER NEEDED A DIVINE INTERVENTION?

OUR SCRIPTURE REFERENCE

In revisiting acts 12:5–11, we can examine this incipient movement called "The Way" and how it experiences exponential growth later. The primary reason or theory, that we have also examined in length, is that some in the church had gone beyond the comfort zone by taking the Gospel beyond the Jews. In the text and in what we've learned, the church decides to move beyond their comfort zone, and they find, in return, that the hand of the Lord is with them. And, subsequently, many turn to the Lord and believe in the Gospel. Some segments of the church soon discover that going beyond their own comfort levels in ministry caused them to experience the presence, power, and participation of God in some very unique ways. In applying this to real life in the ensuing chapters, we have established that stepping out of tried and true comfort zones is often a good thing in furthering our lives, our success, and our relationships with people and places. We can learn divine things from these simple steps in reaching out. We'll learn, here, how to recognize and accept divine intervention—even in those times when we might not be ready to see it.

In our discussion, thus far, the old church is growing and prospering. Later, however, the opposition rises again. We have seen, in the book of Acts, over and over, that as the ministry grows, so does the potential for opposition. Growth and opposition occur in tandem. And, we also know this to be true in real life. Often, when ministry, success, numbers, involvement is growing and prospering, we hear the "squeaky wheels"—the naysayers. Therefore, logically, we would, then, only read of the opposition rearing its ugly head when the church is moving forward. The movement of the church activates the opposition of the enemy. The enemy lies dormant until movement begins—positive movement—movement to create change or, many times, inclusion. The moment a church decides to launch out on a project, a new ministry, a building endeavor, or some innovative initiative, expectations for the enemy to rise are there. If there is no opposition, it probably means there is no positive change. In life, we have a tendency to lay low and attempt to stay dormant, so that we do not invite opposition or create the opportunity to have to defend our actions and ourselves. From the simplest gestures—like asking a new neighbor to lunch with an already established group of friends —to the larger ones—like suggesting that the church take a new direction, we have all felt that push back.

THE BIBLICAL TEXT FOR THIS ANALYSIS

In revisiting the text, we find that Herod decides to execute James, the brother of John. When he sees that this act boosted his national approval ratings, he decides to do the same to Peter. However, he cannot execute Peter immediately, because it was the Passover season when Peter was apprehended. So, he imprisons Peter until he can execute him without causing uproar. The great irony here is that Herod probably should have gotten rid of him while he had a chance. Herod's delay provided—not only space for push and opposition of a positive nature—it opened the door for divine intervention! And, how many of us desire to have that type of intervention in our lives on a daily basis? After all, we pray for strength, more money, loved ones to recover from illness, but... do we always see such immediate results? Or, do we just need to look closer?

DO WE REALLY KNOW WHAT IT'S LIKE TO BE "IN JAIL"?

Peter is in jail. He is awaiting what, in all probability, will be his death. Peter is in a jail—a physical jail. Now, in spiritually examining our own lives, how many of us are in prisons, which no one can see—intellectual, emotional, or spiritual prisons? A few years ago, Jovan Belcher, a successful Kansas City Chiefs football player who appeared to have a great career, a loving family, and a lot to live for, ended up shooting and killing his live-in girlfriend. He, then, drove to the parking lot of the Arrowhead football stadium and shot himself. Commenting on this tragedy, one of Belcher's teammates said, "Jovan was dealing with something that none of us could see." By this, he meant that as friends and family struggled to make sense of the tragedy, we have to think that he was tortured. He was in a prison that we couldn't see. He wasn't in a physical prison that we could see and understand; he was in some kind of invisible prison. He was wrestling with something that only he knew about. Maybe it is not that extent for most of us—maybe our demons are not that overwhelming, but there are scores of people who are incarcerated in the invisible cells of their own psyches. We sing and shout in our worship, but I often wonder, as a pastor, who is locked up today—in my congregation? Everyone shows up dressed to impress, but I wonder who is suffering—who needs my help (or someone else's) the most? People say to us, "how are you doing?" And we say, "fine…" But, I wonder how many of us are incarcerated on a daily basis. "Yes there's a smile on my face, but it's only there to fool the public, but when it comes down to fooling you, well that's a different subject… The tears of a clown, when there's no one around…" (Smokey Robinson and the Miracles, Tamla Records, a subsidiary of Motown, 1967.)

As you listen to this, readers, I'm sure you all feel that you can recognize when someone is in trouble or when you, yourself, need to step back and take stock of your situation—your depression—your happiness—or… other issues. But, can we always do that? Is it always easy to tell if someone is hurting so badly that he or she feels like it is a prison from which there is no escape? Can we tell the difference in our own lives and families whether or not the problems we have are problems like any other or special ones from which we may not recover? If we can tell, what do we do? How do we help our situation or the situation of another?

So, again, Peter was in jail, but we are about to see a turning point to this story. In fact, in the story of anyone's deliverance, there is a turning point; there is that moment when something happens which turns the tide. The turning point for Peter is in verse five: "so Peter was kept in prison, but the church was earnestly praying to God for him." The turning point is in the prayer. While the enemy was working on one side, the people of God were working on the other side. The only thing they had to combat the enemy was prayer. The enemy had resources. Herod had the backing of Rome. Herod had the backing of the ecclesiastical authorities. The only thing the church had was prayer. But, maybe that's all the church needed. All they had was all they needed. Sometimes what you think is all you have may be all you need! This is a point that we can all learn from. In the tragic story that we examined earlier, we heard that a man was suffering beyond what we could understand. If someone could have intervened and made him see all that he possessed that was good, maybe tragedy could be averted. If we just look to that person sitting next to us in Sunday worship, maybe we could avert a tragedy—make someone's day—change a life.

The only thing they had to combat the enemy was prayer.

THE TURNING POINT IN ANY CRISIS IS PRAYER

Prayer is often taken for granted. It is seen as the last resort. It is ignored as though it is antiquated and outdated. But, it is the key to the turning point. The church gathers in prayer, and that's when everything gets started. Prayer is always starting something. If you want to get something started, pray! I know how it sounds. It sounds too juvenile; it sounds too ordinary, but the key to getting something started is on your knees in prayer. Yes, God frees Peter from jail, but nothing got started until the church prayed. At the foundation of deliverance was prayer. As Thomas Watson, the Puritan preacher said, "the angel fetched Peter out of jail; but prayer is what fetched the angel." If you want to "fetch" God, you need to pray. Once they called on the Lord, deliverance became a reality.

Prayer is often taken for granted.

This deliverance is INTERNAL BEFORE IT IS EXTERNAL. You feel it or understand it—know, inherently, what it is you need to extricate yourself from your troubles—before it actually happens—before you actually see or feel the help that you know is coming. In the text, it was the night before Peter was to stand trial. The death sentence was being held over him. His life was hanging in the balance. Obviously, Peter had heard about the execution of James and knew it was a real possibility for him. That night Peter was chained to two soldiers. One was on one side and the other on the other side. Another squad of soldiers was at the door. Herod put Peter under maximum security, because Peter had escaped from jail before. Herod was not taking any chances. There were a total of sixteen soldiers guarding Peter in shifts of four. Herod knew he couldn't be comfortable with the fact that Peter was in jail.

All of this overwhelming detail is surrounding Peter. Death, soldiers, the prison bars, and uncertainty are all staring him in the face. Yet, when we find Peter, he is asleep between the soldiers. He is asleep! How do you sleep at a time like this? You are locked up and you don't know the outcome of the circumstance. You still don't know how the marriage is going to turn out. You are still waiting for the test results from the doctor. You don't know if the job is yours. You still don't know if the money is coming thru. You don't know when the pain will ease up. How can you sleep at a time like that? He should have been pacing the floors. He should have been asking for a drink. He should have been looking for some kind of sleeping pill. He should have been stressed out, tossing and turning. Instead, he is asleep. Like Daniel was sleeping in the lion's den in the face of the lions, Peter was asleep in this jail cell. Like Jesus was asleep on the boat when the waves were tossing into the boat, Peter was asleep. Peter was asleep right in the face of the enemy. They were probably wondering how he could sleep. Can you sleep in the face of your troubles? With your issues staring you in the face—can you rest? And, the truth is if you know how to offset your troubles—your enemy—your lion in the room—your soldiers on both sides—you can rest easy too. If you know where to turn, how to fix your issues, and what to do—whether that is turning to God or relying on family—or gathering all your fortitude and resources to face financial or professional hardship or —making a call to a therapist or friends to face personal trouble—you can handle it all and sleep like you have no troubles—live like you have a clear vision for success and the future.

Why was Peter able to sleep in the face of what he was facing? Perhaps one reason is that this was not the first time he had been in these circumstances. In Acts 5:17, Peter and the other apostles were in jail and an angel freed him. He's not panicking, because this is not the first time he's been in this kind of trouble. He had been there and done that. He knew that God had come through before. He knew that God had opened doors before. It would probably help me to sleep if I remembered that some of the things that are facing me, I've been in before. I need to recognize that this is not the first time I've been sick. This is not the first time I was facing surgery. This is not the first time I've been broke! Peter had experience in the area of persecution and imprisonment. Thus, he was able to rest; he was able to sleep even when his troubles were staring him in the face!

Perhaps he was able to sleep between two soldiers because the church was praying for him. The church, which was gathered at Sister Mary's house, was praying in one place, but perhaps the impact was being felt in another place. Maybe their prayers had brought calm to Peter, and Peter did not even know why. Before prayer did anything about what he was in, maybe prayer did something about what was in him. Prayer brought calm before it brought change. And Peter did not even know why. Sometimes you are making it based on the prayers of some folks who are not even around you. Sometimes you experience a calm out of nowhere, and you don't even know why. It could be that somebody, somewhere is praying just for you. You get peace of out nowhere; you get joy out of nowhere; you are able to press on out of nowhere. It could be that a network of prayer is being offered for you.

It could be that somebody, somewhere is praying just for you.

Why is Peter able to sleep? It could be that he recalled the word spoken to him by Jesus. In John 21:18,19. There, Jesus tells Peter about what will happen to him when he is old. At this point in his life, while he is in jail, Peter is still relatively young. If the word of the Lord is true, Peter is going to live on until he his older. So no matter how things look for him, he trusts what he has heard. If God's word is true, then something is going to happen between that night and the time of his execution. Peter is able to sleep, because he is trusting in God's Word. What he sees in life looks much different than what he heard in the Word. But, the only way he can rest is if he relies on what he heard in the Word. If you want to be able to sleep in the face of your troubles, you have to believe what you've heard and not just what you see. What he sees are the soldiers. What he sees are the threats of Herod. What he sees are the chains. But, what he heard is that the Lord will make a way somehow! Can you trust what you've heard? "Tis so sweet to trust in Jesus, just to take Him at His word! Just to REST upon His promise. Just to know it was said by God…"

READER'S PAUSE

LIVING WELL: WHAT DOES DIVINE INTERVENTION MEAN TO YOU?

We all pray for help now and then. We all need strength and often draw on God for it. What exactly does "divine intervention" mean to you? Is it appropriate to ask God for things? Or, is it more appropriate or right to ask God for the fortitude and necessary tools to make it through this life? Explain your thoughts/answer here:

The bottom-line is that Peter was delivered internally before he was delivered externally. Even before he was freed from his circumstances, he was freed from his circumstances. Peter was victorious even though life had not changed. So that even if the circumstances had not changed, he was still the victor. He was the victor, because he was able to overcome the fear associated with what he was going through. If I can rise above the fear of what I am in, I actually become the victor. When you let remembrance put you to sleep; when you let prayer put you to sleep; and when you let trust put you to sleep in the face of uncertainty, you become the victor. Real deliverance starts on the inside before anything changes on the outside.

RE-EXAMINING OUR TEXT IN CONTEXT

This text teaches us that deliverance is internal before it is external. It also teaches us that DELIVERANCE IS INCLUSIVE OF YOUR PARTICIPATION. Peter was asleep so soundly that the angel, who had interrupted the night, had to hit Peter on the side. The angel "struck him." This was no gentle wake-up call. He had to hit him. After he hit him, he said, "Quick, get up." And then the text says, "and the chains fell off Peter's wrists." Something is happening here. First of all, how do you tell a man who is chained to two soldiers to get up? He can't get up. In the next breath, it says "and the chains fell off Peter's wrists…" I don't know how the sequence of events occurred. But, it is implied that the chains only fall off because Peter decides to get up. Maybe the chains only fall off because he makes some attempt to get up. Maybe there are certain chains, which do not fall off of us until we decide to make a move. Perhaps effort in the direction of deliverance accelerates deliverance. Maybe the Lord just wants a move toward deliverance on our part, and then some chains will begin to fall off. Maybe there are still some chains on me, because I refuse to get up. As I move, God liberates. As I move, God gets active. I can't sit around and wait for the chains to fall off. I have to make a move in the direction of my liberation. It may be nothing but a single decision to change. It may take just one moment of saying "no", which will turn me in the direction of deliverance.

The angel says, "Quick—get up", and the chains fell off of Peter! Maybe the chains had already been loosed, but they don't fall off until Peter decides to get up! There are some things that I have been freed from, and I don't even know because I'm still living like I've been locked up. Maybe, readers, you feel the same way at times. We don't always know if our support is truly in place. Am I ready to move? Am I ready to make things better? Am I ready to test my faith in God and move this issue out of my life? Getting up will confirm that I've been free, and the same will follow for all of you. If you go ahead and start living—if you go ahead and start getting active again—you may discover that you are over it! Quit being locked from what you need to free yourself from! If we take the steps to help our own situation and believe divine intervention—believe our own power to overcome—tap into the resources we have—we CAN overcome a lot in life. In fact, if we understand our own potential and the fact that God does give us what we need, we can overcome most obstacles.

If we understand our own potential and the fact that God does give us what we need, we can overcome most obstacles.

Again, Peter gets up, and the angel tells him to get dressed. The angel says, "Put your sandals and clothes on and follow me." Peter is still in prison, but the angel tells him to dress for freedom. He is yet in jail, but he needs to get dressed for where he is headed and not for where he is. Being almost naked was ok for jail, but it wasn't ok for where God was taking him. So, he needed to get dressed for the next level—just like we all need to dress or prepare for these moments in our own lives. He needed to look like he was prepared to move out of his current situation. Readers, we all need to take heed here. Make sure that you feel, look, and project the part you want. Do you want to move out of your troubles? Do you want to do so in confidence? Then, clothe yourself—prepare yourself—for your task. Get dressed and start looking like yourself—like someone in control who knows where God is taking you. Start dressing like the job is yours. Start smiling like the doors have already been open. Start looking ahead like you can already see your future, and it will be yours.

Now, it is important to note in the text that the angel loosens the chains and unlocks doors, but he doesn't put Peter's shoes on for him. God will do the extraordinary, but he will not do the ordinary. He will not do what we are capable of doing ourselves. The Lord is not going to unlock the doors and clothe Peter. He is going to answer his prayers—our prayers—provide divine intervention for all who seek it and help themselves in some way—show faith in daily life. There are some things that you have to do in your own deliverance, however. Divine deliverance requires human cooperation. The Lord did call Lazarus from the grave, but the people did have to roll the stone away themselves. Jesus did feed over five thousand, but the disciples did have to go throughout the crowd to find anyone who has food first. The Lord did heal the man who was born blind, but he did have to stumble his way to the Pool of Siloam. God is able to deliver me from unemployment, but He is not going to go look for a job for me. God is able to heal a broken relationship, but He is not going to go to counseling for me. A lot of this we have to do for ourselves in order to achieve what we are meant for—for which we are destined. In this case, Peter's obedience and participation are necessary if he is going to be freed. He has to follow the instructions of the angel. Deliverance is not always mystical and miraculous. There are some very ordinary elements to deliverance. Deliverance is sometimes about painful, hard-nosed obedience.

Deliverance is sometimes about painful, hard-nosed obedience.

Divine deliverance is internal before it is external, it is inclusive of your participation, and it is also IMPERCEPTIBLE TO THE ENEMY. The angel leads Peter through the prison without anyone knowing it. He gets him from between the two guards who are chained to him, and they don't know it. He leads Peter through the first set of guards who are guarding the jail, and they don't know it. He leads Peter through the second set of guards, and they don't know it. They get to the gates to the city, and they don't have to climb it; they don't have to try to force their way through. The door opens for them. Some deliverance is loud and dramatic; sometimes it is quiet and subtle. It is very interesting that all of this is happening during the celebration of Passover. Passover is the recollection and celebration of the sea opening up and the people of God making it out of Egyptian bondage. Now Peter is experiencing his own personal "exodus." What God does on a "macro" level, God can do on a "micro level." What God can do for the people, God can do for you in your own circumstances. God can handle "macro" issues like opening up seas for thousands, and God candle "micro" issues like opening up prison doors for just one. Bring God your "macro" issues and your "micro" issues! He's not just the God of big seas; He's also the God of small cell doors.

Now, let's note: God does this right under the nose of those who are guarding Peter. God does this right under the nose of those who believe Peter is still locked up. The Lord frees Peter at night; the enemy doesn't know it till the morning. God acts at night, the people discover it in the morning. God acts in the shroud of darkness. You go into bed at night and see what God can do at night. God does some of His best work at night! At night, the Lord smote the firstborn of Egypt. At night God rocked the jail where Paul and Silas were imprisoned.

YOU KNOW GOD, BUT DO YOU REALLY RECOGNIZE HIM?

People don't always know how nor when God is freeing them or anyone else. They might not recognize it in their own lives; they might not know it has happened to you or others. The only thing that they can see is that your mood is better, your step is quicker, your back is straighter, and your life is better. They can see you have a new level of joy—you're worshipping better—looking better—and loving life. And even if they don't know why, they do know that the Lord has opened up doors for you. They can assume that there has been some sort of divine intervention and that you have taken it and run with it—seized the opportunities put before you. They don't know that God has moved some mountains or has given you strength to climb them. They don't know that God has been the lifter of your head! You know, however, and that is what is important—what will continue to motivate you.

Divine Deliverance is internal before it is external; it is inclusive of your participation, imperceptible to the enemy, and inspiring of testimony to the Lord. Once Peter is led outside of the city gate, the angel leaves him. The work of the angel is over. The manifested presence of the Lord will not be a crutch for Peter. Peter is suddenly on his own. What will he do with his liberation? What will he do with his freedom? First of all, we know that he comes to his own realization. He says, "Now I know…" After having been freed there are some things he knows now that did not know before! All of us should have that testimony at some point. "Now I know…" After you are freed—after you are liberated—after the Lord brings you out of some things, which you could not get yourself out of, you ought to be able to say, "Now I know…" There are some things, which you did not know twenty years ago; but "now you know…" I used to hear my daddy and some seasoned preachers during the conclusion of the sermons talking about "He is a way out of no way. He is a bridge of troubled waters. He is a doctor in a sickroom…" I used to say those things when I first started preaching, because they sounded good. But "now I know..." I finally understand what I was actually saying—what I was preaching—what I had heard all those years. Do you know anything now that you did not know then? And how have you used that knowledge? How WILL you use that knowledge?

WHAT PETER SAYS TO US

What do you know, Peter? Peter says, "I know that the Lord rescued me..." I know I was in something that I couldn't get myself out of. This is what you ought to know after you've been liberated. You ought to know that if I had not been for the Lord on your side... You ought to know that "no weapon formed against you shall prosper..." You ought to know that it was not your wit that got you out; it was not your good looks that got you out; it was not your money that got you out of some circumstances. It was the power of the Lord!

Peter then went to the people who had been praying for him and showed himself to them. He goes to the home of sister Mary, and he knocks on the door until they know it's him. The Lord had done too much for him for him to keep a secret. The deliverance was secret, but the praise is in front of everybody. God made a way in private, but glory for Him will be in the presence of all the people. When the Lord has brought you out, go tell somebody! Make His praise glorious. Make his praise loud! You were created to make His praise glorious.

When the Lord has brought you out, go tell somebody!

CASE STUDY 2

STEPPING OUT OF OUR COMFORT ZONE, TAKING OUR FAITH WITH US, AND FINALLY UNDERSTANDING DIVINE DELIVERANCE

We've established, in the preceding chapters, that stepping out of our comfort zone is not always easy. Neither is always feeling our faith and touting it in situations outside of Sunday worship. And, above all, accepting or recognizing divine intervention and running with it to achieve success in life is daunting as well. It is not in our nature, as humans, to change our routine or step out of the tried and true. And, even if we have strong faith, talking about it and arguing it in situations outside worship feel strange. Of course, we all know that, even if we want divine intervention, we don't always feel it or understand it—or—and this is the most difficult to accept—we don't always take the opportunity to better ourselves or use the tools God has given us to make our lives better.

Expectations are strange in many ways. Knowing friends and family for a long time, we expect certain behaviors, and we even take some for granted. One day, after I had been in my office working on next Sunday's sermon, I encountered a young man sitting and waiting to speak to me. I recognized him because I knew his family, but he wasn't a churchgoer, and he didn't know me personally. I knew he was, basically, a good kid—had played basketball—got pretty good grades—had a girlfriend who did go to church, but I knew he ran, on occasion, with a rougher group of guys—some of them known for trouble. He seemed nervous but approached me in earnest. He asked if we could talk.

When he began his story, I sensed that he was off his game a bit—felt uncomfortable—seemed to want to leave. He told me that he had been given a recent business opportunity that his mother did not approve of. Beyond that, he felt that this opportunity warranted him dropping out of high school. When he had told his mother his plans, she had make it clear to him that he would, then, be on his own. If he was not going to take the time and care to finish high school and help himself—after all her hard work—then, he would have to make it work—this new job / new life—on his own. His girlfriend felt the same way, and his basketball coach had flat out told him that he was ruining his chances for a college scholarship. Still, he felt he needed to do this—could not let his friends down—could not leave this group of peers who had offered him the "job".

I didn't ask him what the "job" was; I simply asked him to reflect on this opportunity and what it meant to him and to his loved ones. I asked him to pray for an answer—to pray for strength to do the right thing. He told me that he didn't pray and had only come to me because he knew his mother and his girlfriend respected me and attended church every Sunday. I told him to reflect on that too—to ask himself why he had come to me—why he was questioning his decision. He left, and I returned to my work. Within a few hours, however, he was back. He told me that he had decided to forgo the offer. Beyond that, he said that his coach, prompted by his meeting with him, had pushed him to contact a respected college regarding his basketball. His girlfriend, also prompted by the conversation, had encouraged him to go to church. And his mother, again encouraged by her need to offset this questionable "job" prospect, had spoken to another family member about a lucrative job for him. I asked him what he was going to do about it all, and he said that he had never felt a divine intervention before. But, in almost making a big mistake in joining a less than desirable group of peers on a questionable "job"—one that may have lead him to destruction, he had felt it. He felt the Lord speak to him, telling him to reach out—leave his comfort zone and look to others for answers. In doing this—in trying to better his own situation—push himself a little while staying open to answers, he found his way—and it was a successful way—one with a potentially deeply satisfying future. I felt that I had not done much to help him, but I did note the lesson—both for him and for myself.

And now, while I have the attention of my valued readers, I want to encourage all of you to look beyond yourselves—look past what you think it comfortable or easy—and... try to see your own potential. Leave your eyes and your heart open, and God will tell you what you need to do to make your life the best it can be.

7

A WONDERFUL CHANGE

(LIVING BEYOND THE LABEL) ACTS 2:14a

OUR SCRIPTURE REFERENCE

In Acts 2:14a, the disciples were told to wait. As anxious as they were to get started with living, they were told to wait. As anxious as they were to get the news out, they were told to wait. As much as they thought they were ready to go to the next level, they were told to wait. They were told to wait based on a promise.

Have we ever, in our own lives, been held to this type of waiting? Have we imposed it on ourselves or had it imposed upon us? Maybe we had to wait for a promotion or work on a project before we got paid. Maybe it was hard to wait for a wedding day or another celebration of sorts. And, did we view this "waiting" as an imposition or did we accept it as part of the ebb and flow of life? I know it is not easy to wait when we're looking forward to something, nor is it easy to wait when we're worried about something or anticipating something for a variety of reasons. Many times, however, the waiting is warranted or will lead to something better.

And, as we've explored in previous chapters, God does truly work in mysterious ways, and these reasons are not always apparent to us right away. The important lesson here is, however, to wait when God asks you to. Often, only He knows what is in store.

God does truly work in mysterious ways, and these reasons are not always apparent to us right away.

PUTTING OUR LIVES ON HOLD UNTIL GOD TELLS US TO MOVE

We know that the post-resurrected Christ had a conversation with the disciples during a forty-day period between resurrection and ascension. In this conversation, He told His disciples to stay in Jerusalem. Jerusalem was where they were hiding out during the tumultuous time of the crucifixion and its aftermath. Jerusalem was the place where they could be in danger themselves, yet He told them to stay there until the promise of the gift from the Father was fulfilled. He said, "stay in Jerusalem" = yet, again, Jerusalem had been the place of their disappointment and of their shattered dreams. And, when Jesus tells them to stay at that place, He does say that the place of their disappointment would also be the place of their breakthrough. He assures them that the place of their crisis would also be the place of their change, and the location of their misery would be the birthplace of their ministry.

"Don't move", He said. "Put your lives on hold." There are many things and people for whom putting your life on hold may not be such a wise thing. But, when it comes to God and God's promises, it is worth putting your life on hold. If God promises you something, you can count on it! God does not make promises, which He cannot keep. If God puts your life on hold, it's because he is getting you ready for what is around the corner. Jesus tells the disciples to "sit". It is difficult to sit when you think you are ready for the next level—ready to move on. But if God says, "sit", you might want to relax until God does what God needs to do. Again, in the case of the disciples, He tells them to wait there because the same way John baptized people in water, they were going to be baptized with the Spirit in just a few days. The same way they were covered with water in water baptism, they were going to be covered in the presence, power, and person of the Holy Spirit.

If God promises you something, you can count on it!

This was the promise, and this is exactly what happened. It was on the day of Pentecost. God moved on this holy day. The Spirit came. The Spirit fell upon all 120 of them who were gathered in that place. As a powerful wind, the Spirit came. As intense fire, the Spirit came. All of those who were gathered, upon whom the Spirit fell, began to speak in different languages. Because it was Pentecost, there were many different types of people from various nations present in Jerusalem. Arabs were there. Italians were there. Asians were there. Africans were there. The miracle is that they all heard these disciples speaking in their own languages. The real miracle of Pentecost was the hearing, not necessarily the speaking.

READER'S PAUSE

LIVING WELL: MAKING POSITIVE CHANGES IN LIFE

When, in your life, have you made a significant positive change in your life or the life of another? Tell your story here:

____

____

____

____

What, in the future, do you think you can do to change your neighborhood, your church, a conflict in your family, or even a world issue? Detail your thoughts here with a tentative timeline for execution of this grand plan.

____

____

____

WOULD YOU BELIEVE THE "SPEAKING IN TONGUES" STORY IF YOU HEARD IT?

These foreign visitors to the city started asking, "What does this mean?" They didn't know what to make of it. Some of them, however, started mocking the disciples and claimed that they had had too much wine. These are folks who did not have a category for what they observed, and, therefore, came to their own ignorant conclusions. These are folks who were not a part of this praise moment, thus it was easy for them to trivialize what had happened. They saw people shouting, running, speaking, and praising God, and it created a sense of awkwardness for them, and, therefore, they trivialized it. There are some people who do not know what to do with praise, and they do not know what to do at the moment praise erupts. Therefore, they have to attribute it to something other than what it is. They have to come up with their own explanations in order to tolerate it. They say, "They're just being emotional." They say, "They're just ignorant. All that noise is not necessary." When people are in the midst of praise and worship, it is not appropriate to trivialize it by talking to them or to crack jokes about it. In fact, it is never appropriate to allow your discomfort to disrupt the worship of another. And, further, don't trivialize praise by analyzing it. These outsiders tried to explain the miracle away by attributing it to something carnal. There are people who are not used to the miraculous, and they will attempt to explain your miracles away. We all have to know how to ignore that and be honest about what we know God has done in our lives. No matter what someone says, we have to declare, with frequency, that, "if it had not been for the Lord who was on your side…" We have to also declare; "I will lift up mine eyes to the hills from whence comes my help... My help comes from the Lord." Don't allow people to explain away your miracles!

Don't allow people to explain away your miracles!

Now, again, in examining what the disciples went through, Peter hears this mocking, and he responds. Peter says, "No, no, no these folks have not been drinking. They are not drunk like you assume they are. They are intoxicated, but not with the substance you are thinking of. They are, in fact, full of the Holy Spirit." Peter goes on to say, "this is that..." To be clear, he is implying that the actions the outsiders observed were explained by the prophecy of Joel, who said that the day was coming when the Lord was going to pour out his Spirit upon all people. Peter is saying this is that same Spirit. Underneath it all, "this" is "that." The only way for them to understand "this", they would need to be in touch with "that". People who are not in touch with "that" would not understand "this." You can't expect folks who do not know the Spirit to be able to understand the move of the Spirit. Peter goes on to preach the Gospel, and he extends an invitation. With that invitation, three thousand people come to Christ and unite with the church. After his sermon, people make a decision for the Lord. The Gospel demands a decision!

Certainly, most of us, readers, consider ourselves faithful or churchgoers in some way. I'm wondering, however, if any of us ever decided to accept God and His Gospel into our lives or did we just accept the fact that our families were churchgoers or that we were in a certain community and, so, we chose a certain church? Did we put our own decision to the test or did we simply learn by habit or through family and friends to go to a certain church and sit and listen to the message every week? If we had to choose, I wonder what message we would lean towards or would we change anything about our current paths—even begin preaching and ministering to others a bit more or mesh that message with what is happening in our own lives. Would we take what we've learned and give it to others? Would we use life experience to bring another message from God through us? Would we change at all? Choice, change, and decision-making are all powerful catalysts for an enriched faith life. We need to pay attention to these messages that come to us.

Choice, change, and decision-making are all powerful catalysts for an enriched faith life.

Peter's message was amazing! The fact that all these people end up coming to the Lord is amazing. But, the most amazing thing to me in this whole scenario is in the first four words in v.14: "then Peter stood up..." What amazes me is that he "stood up." He stands up before the eleven others stand up. Peter takes the initiative. In times past, Peter would have denied that he even knew anything about what was happening. But—here—he takes a stand when in other times he would have shut up. What amazes me is "how he stood up." He stood up with a gentle spirit. He starts with, "fellow Jews..."—and, in this, there is a sense of mellowness in his response. In times past, he might have been hostile or lashed out at others. What amazes me is what comes out of him when he speaks—gentleness and approachability. Not long after he opens his mouth, the

Word of God comes out. He quotes one of the Minor Prophets—and, again, stays gentle and approachable. In times past, Peter might have had less than kind words for people. In fact, at one time, no one could predict what Peter was going to say. But… something had changed him.

THE POSSIBILITIES BROUGHT ON BY CHANGE

There had been a great change in Peter. Everyone knew how Peter had messed up. I'm sure that Peter had been labeled based on his mistakes, and society rarely lets anyone live beyond labels. Once someone has been labeled, that's it. We don't believe people can change. Hence, we always claim we know someone based on what he or she has done. However, we don't know how the Lord has been working in someone's life! We have to be careful attaching labels to people because we will, then, never give them space to change. Whatever they do or say will be discounted because of the perceived label already attached to him or her. Someone could have already become a butterfly, but because we once saw him or her as a caterpillar, that's the way he or she will always be perceived. Everyone will ignore the beauty of their wings, because we are stuck with the image of them crawling around on the ground—that caterpillar that we all thought they were. And we need to note this; we have to be careful attaching labels to people, because change is possible in the kingdom of God. With God, people can change. With God, you are not bound to who or what you have been. Possibilities are endless with the Lord. With God, "shall be is always a possibility."

And so we see this change in Peter. And, we should note this change because others are capable of change, and we are capable of change. Peter stood up. He stood up, because he had grown up. He probably didn't even know how much he had grown up until this situation forced him to stand up. You may not know how much you've grown up until you're forced to stand up. Life will show you how much you've grown. In fact, life will either show you how much more you need to grow or how much you have grown. You may not know how far along you've come until life shows you. You don't demonstrate how much you've grown in the Lord in the comfort of the sanctuary. You don't know how far along you've come until you've been tested in a certain area—something out of your realm—with something that challenges you. We would have never known how much Peter had developed if these outsiders had never accused Peter and his folks of being drunk. It is how Peter responds to an accusation—it is how Peter responds to people talking about him and the other believers which shows how far along he has come. How we respond to what people say about us says a whole lot about how we've grown in the Lord. They caught Peter at the right time, because they don't know the trouble they could have been in had they been messing with Peter just a month or two earlier! And, sometimes, the Lord chooses when to make the change apparent to everyone.

Peter stood up, because he was not worried about what they thought about him. Some of the people around him, particularly in the company of the 120, knew about Peter's failures. However, he didn't allow their knowledge of his failures to keep him from contributing to the kingdom of God. If they had issues with him standing up after what he had done, that was their issue and not his. We can't always allow people's issues with us to become our issues. We will be in shackles forever if we are operating based on how we think other people perceive us based on our failures. This wasn't about Peter being reckless and simply not caring about what people thought about him. He had repented. He and the Lord had dealt with his fall, so now he was willing to stand up, even with the baggage of his failures. When we know we have dealt with things with the Lord, we go ahead and stand up and contribute. I'm sure that in the secret chambers of his heart, he still dealt with the regrets of his failure. However, he did not allow that the keep him from contributing to the kingdom. He got up and preached Jesus anyway.

CHANGE AS METAMORPHOSIS

Further, Peter stood up because there had been a great change. What led to this change? What was at the bottom of this metamorphosis? His ENCOUNTERS WITH THE RESURRECTED LORD led to this change. Peter's turnaround commenced with the revelation that Jesus is alive! In the Bible, we know that after the resurrection, the Lord appears to His disciples. For forty days He keeps appearing unto them, giving them proof of life. He gives them "convincing proofs" that He is alive. In Mark's Gospel, the angels tell the women who have come to the tomb to anoint the body of Jesus that "He 's not here. Come see where He was lying." And then they go on to say "to tell His disciples and Peter that He is alive and that He is going ahead of them to meet them in Galilee. The resurrected Lord had a special word for Peter. Peter had messed up big time. The resurrection of Christ is big news for people who have messed up big time! Therefore, the post-resurrection encounters for Peter had special significance.

A WONDERFUL CHANGE

Encounters with the resurrected Lord are life changing. Our lives can't help but be changed when we embrace Jesus Christ, who is the resurrected Lord. Life can't help but to go to a whole new level when we encounter Him. His resurrection means that He has overcome the greatest enemy, which is death. If He has overcome that, then He's able to help you overcome whatever seems to be holding you down. Encounters with the resurrected Lord give you hope about yourself. Liberation is possible. There is life-changing power in the resurrection.

The greatest evidence of the resurrection was not the empty tomb. The greatest evidence of the resurrection was not the folded clothes in the tomb. The greatest evidence of the resurrection was not the report of the women. The greatest evidence of the resurrection was evidenced in the changed lives of the disciples. How does this small band of nervous disciples suddenly become the vehicle through which the "world is turned upside down"? It is because we understand that He is alive. Evidence that Christ is alive is evidence that our lives are worth living—worth changing—worth living the way the Lord wants us to live. There is no way that Peter could be who he became had he not run into the resurrected Lord. There is no way that we would be who we are, or we would be doing what we are doing without having run into the resurrected Lord. We don't have to prove the resurrection; we just have to direct people to the positive changes in our own lives and make known how the Lord has influenced us.

The greatest evidence of the resurrection was evidenced in the changed lives of the disciples.

What exactly lead to this great change in Peter? Not only was it his encounters with the resurrected Lord, but it was also EMPOWERMENT FROM THE SPIRIT. When the Spirit was poured out on the day of Pentecost, it affected all of them. Peter was included. Pentecost, according to theologian James Dunn, ushered in a new age. Dunn says that salvation-history is divided up into the three periods; the period of Israel; the period of Jesus; and the period of the church, which is the era between the ascension of Christ and the second coming of Christ. This is the period of the Holy Spirit working through the church. This period began with the coming of the Spirit. The out-pouring of the Spirit is bigger than a few people speaking in tongues. It is bigger than a mighty rushing wind and ominous fire. This coming of the Spirit is bigger than people shouting. It is the actually the beginning of a new era in God's salvation history. It is the ushering in of a new cosmic age. We need to note this phenomenon and continue to move it forward—note our own changes, celebrate them, and make others aware of the power of God.

This dawning of the new age, cosmically, means the possibilities for newness personally for those who received that Spirit. In the story of Peter and Jesus' ascension, the dawning of the new age was happening in the lives of those who were in that upper room. Peter was there. This was the beginning of something new for Peter. That 's why he was able to stand now where he would have fallen before. He can stand now where he would have fallen before, because of the power of the Spirit. When we look back, I'm sure there are some places where we can stand now where we would have fallen before. Maybe we grew and learned and had no idea that we had transformed in one or other areas of our lives. There are some experiences, which would have knocked us down ten years ago, but we can stand now because of these experiences and learning opportunities with God. There are some troubles (financial, personal, and professional), which would have caused a nervous breakdown years ago, but maybe we can stand now! The power of the Spirit brings strength to stand. Of course, we can stand and withstand some things after Pentecost—after these life-changing experiences with God or with growth through difficulties in live—all of which we couldn't withstand. But because we all now have experienced strength—and understood the impact of the Pentecost, we can now handle.

THE POWER OF RESILIENCE

One of the toys, which used to intrigue me as a boy, was a balloon-like figure that had some sort of clown face on it. You could hit this figure and it would bounce right back up. I couldn't understand that, so I asked my mother about it. She didn't really know either. She simply said, "It's just full of something that makes it stand after it's been hit!" And now—when we are full of the "right stuff", we can stand when we are hit. We might tip over, but we can bounce back up. When you are filled with Spirit, you have newfound strength.

When we are filled with the Spirit, we also have newfound courage and boldness. Peter's stand in this setting is about a newfound courage. The Spirit gives birth to boldness. I've heard that the consumption of alcohol will give you boldness to do and say things you wouldn't ordinarily say or do…that's what I've heard. Something in us takes over, and we get a newfound boldness. It is fitting, to some extent, that the disciples are accused of being drunk, because this new Spirit they have has given them a new boldness. It is true that God has not given us the spirit of fear, but of love, power, and a sound mind. There are some things you can face without fear now, because of the indwelling of the Spirit. No need to be afraid when you've been through Pentecost.

What brought about this change in Peter? It was his encounter with the Savior; it was his empowerment from the Spirit, but it was also THE EDIFICATION FROM THE SAINTS. When Peter stands, he is not standing alone. The eleven stand with him. After people messed up, he left the church. He went off on his own somewhere for a period of time. He felt as though he did not belong with the people of God because of his failure. He disassociated himself from the church because of what he was going through personally. Peter did not realize that whatever he was going through, the church could help him. We need to realize, too, that when we are going through something, that's when we need the church.

At some point, after Jesus had been raised from the dead and after He had found Peter, Peter returns to the body of believers. Peter's life begins to change when he returns to the body of believers. When he returns, that community of faith is not perfect. There are some doubters there. The numbers are incomplete, because Judas is not there. He has committed suicide. This band of believers is still dealing with that. When Peter returns to the church, it is not a perfect place, but nevertheless he needs them. He can't survive and thrive without this community of faith. As time went on, this group of disciples would have some issues with each other. They would fuss and fight here and there. They would disappoint each other; nevertheless they stayed together, because they needed each other. In fact, growth and development occur within the context of the community of faith.

Peter stands with the eleven. No matter how spiritual Peter might be now and no matter how caught up in the Holy Ghost he is, he recognizes that he still needs the eleven, and beyond that—the 120 or whatever his change and his reach entails. We ought not ever get so holy that we feel like we don't need the people of God. After having been filled with the Spirit, it would have been easy for Peter to feel arrogant—almost as though he did not need anybody. But, this is not so; Peter recognizes that he can't make it without Him.

Praise God that the eleven never did allow Peter to stand by himself. Peter faced, to some extent, the opposition. Peter faced something bigger than he could have imagined, and his community would not let him face it alone. In the face of the outsiders, the disciples stand together. In the face of this rumor that they are drunk, they stand together. That fact that they stand with him gives him boldness in this hour. And, we can all experience this in some capacity as we grow and learn with God and accept these changes and challenges that life sends us. Peter had experienced a great change. It was because of the encounters with the Lord, empowerment of the Spirit, and edification from the saints that this change occurred. The Lord changed him. God can do it for you!

8

THE UPSIDE OF TROUBLE

When you're in trouble, it is difficult to think about any so-called upside to the problem. You don't want to hear anyone tell you about the benefits of trouble or adversity. You've heard enough. You just want out! Enough already! You want deliverance. You just want things to get better. I think we all feel the same way.

Regarding trouble and problems, what "upside" could there be to what you—or anybody else—are going through? What upside could there be to being broke? What upside could there be to turbulent or even ruptured relationships? What upside could there be to prolonged illness, doctor's bills, and perpetual pain? What upside could there be to discovering some significant issue with your child or grandchild? I am careful with this subject, because it is so easy to talk about someone else's trouble from a positive perspective. When it's someone else's issue, it's easy to speak about the "upside." When it's someone else's issue, it's easy to tell that person to "just pray." It's easy to send an encouraging text, tweet, or e-mail when it is someone else's trouble. It's hard, however, to locate that "upside" when it is your trouble, when it's your bills, when it's your job search, when it's your marriage, or when it's your child. Recently, as I was contemplating this passage and this subject, I was also overhearing the story on television of Good Morning America's Robin Roberts, who, because of a rare blood disorder, had taken a leave from the show so that she could have a bone marrow transplant procedure. Robin, who had already been through the trauma of breast cancer, was also dealing with the pain, the thoughts of mortality, loss of hair and weight, and all the other things that come along with such an illnesses. I thought to myself that it is easy for me to think about the upside of her struggle—that she had been through worse, had tremendous support, etc.—because it wasn't my struggle; it was hers.

I'm not saying that we're all immune to the pain and suffering of others. I'm simply pointing out how hard it is to empathize when we can't fathom certain pain or how hard it is to understand adversity if we don't have it in our lives or on our radar at all. Of course, we all will experience it at some time. And, as is always the case with God's message, we will not understand how it helps us at the time. Once we experience the fortitude and confidence brought by such pain or adversity, however, we'll know that feeling forever. Once we know how it is to face another trial when one is already behind us, we will be invincible and able to move mountains in our own lives. Many times, without the test of tolerance and strength, we're never able to try those qualities out in other areas of life. Once we accept our adversity as a lesson from which we emerge better, we can do anything.

Once we accept our adversity as a lesson from which we emerge better, we can do anything.

OUR SCRIPTURE REFERENCE

These realities notwithstanding, I have long wanted to wrestle with this idea at length, because there is something that this passage of Scripture-Acts 8:1,4—is saying to us about our experience of adversity. It speaks to us at the core of our troubles. The narrator says, "On that day, a great persecution broke out..." The growth of the movement and the opposition of the enemy were growing in tandem. The wheat and tares were growing together. The angst and irritation of the opposition had been growing, and it "reached a head" on that day. On what day, you ask? Whatever happened on that "day" is what sparked the persecution. On that day, the opposition of this incipient movement called the "way" was angered by the declaration of Stephen. Stephen ended up preaching a sermon in response to the enemies of the faith bringing him up on charges of blasphemy against the Law of Moses. On that fateful day, he was brought before the high priest. Once there, he took the opportunity to preach the Word of God. At the end of this sermon, Stephen tells the audience that they are "stiff-necked, stubborn, and unspiritual." And then, Stephen starts "playing the dozens," because he actually goes on to talk about their forefathers who killed the prophets whom God sent to them. As if that's not enough, he further tells them that they betrayed and murdered Jesus. As if that's not enough, he tells them that they, themselves, obeyed the very law they are accusing him of not honoring. That's not the kind of preaching that will get you invited to the White House. Those are not the kind of sermons, which will make it to the New York Times Best Sellers list. That's not the kind of preaching that will get a preacher major appointments on significant stages. They heard this and were ready to kill him and stamp out this whole Christian movement. Stephen's mouth helped to create this volatile situation, and he did it deliberately.

WHAT REALLY HAPPENS TO US IN TIMES OF ADVERSITY?

What also really happened on that big day? Not only were they angered by the declaration of Stephen, but they were also astonished by the death of Stephen. They weren't astonished by the fact that he died, because they were the ones who sentenced him to death and killed him. They were astonished by how he died. He died with a testimony on his lips. As they are stoning him, he kept up his testimony—that the heavens opened up and he saw beautiful things. He looks up, and he tells them that he sees the glory of God. Perhaps he could only see brilliant brightness of God's glory because of the opaque darkness of his painful circumstances, but, nevertheless, he looks up and sees the Son of God standing on the right hand of the throne of God. Christ is standing as if to say "I'm able to get to where you are if necessary." Stephen dies with prayer on his lips. What the enemy has done to him has literally knocked him to his knees. While on his knees, he asks the Lord to receive his spirit. What really mattered to him would be in the hands of the Lord. They could take his body but not his spirit. They could have his flesh but not his essential self. There would be some things that he would only put in the hands of the Lord. So Stephen died with a testimony on his lips—he died with prayer on his lips—but he also died with forgiveness on his lips. As he was breathing his last breath, he said, "Lord, do not hold this sin against them…" As they are aiming violence and hatred toward him, Stephen is aiming forgiveness toward them. Stephen refuses to allow them to dictate how he will respond toward them. He rises above how they are treating him. He commits himself to acting and not just reacting. They are controlling what is happening to him, but he will control how he responds. He will not allow bitterness to take him over. He will not stoop to the level of those inflicting so much pain and behaving so badly. None of us should ever alter our faith and our good behavior to mimic those who inflict the pain.

None of us should ever alter our faith and our good behavior to mimic those who inflict the pain.

The enemy sees this and can't stand it. And this is the truth to this day; our enemies cannot handle it when we refuse to act like they act. The enemy wants to fight, but when we refuse to fight the way the enemy fights, the enemy can't take it. When we rise above another's behavior, we invite more anger—more contempt and jealousy—and more confusion. That's why on that day with Stephen, a great persecution broke out. Stephen's reaction to what these people were doing to him showed them that they had lost this fight. The enemy was nervous. Saul, who would later become Paul, was there observing this whole episode, and he, like the rest of them, became nervous. They were nervous, because they knew that there was something to this event—this act that Stephen had executed. Miraculously, Stephen had demonstrated love toward them.

He didn't demonstrate a weak, sentimental love—but, instead, he showed a courageous love, one which does not fight the way the enemy fights. The opposition was truly intimidated by this love. The opposition was not intimidated by revenge and resentment; those are the characteristics that were expected—even understood. The opposition was intimidated by the refusal to be as vindictive and hateful as they were and that will always be the case—with Stephen and with us now.

All hell broke out on that day. To bring it present day, the enemy put a "full court press" on Stephen, just as our favorite basketball teams do to one another now, because it knew it had lost this battle. "On that day", a great persecution broke out against the church at Jerusalem, and all, except the apostles, were scattered…" The persecution dislocated them. The persecution forced them to move beyond where they were. They had to leave Jerusalem—not sure what form this persecution took, but it was enough to force them to disperse. The irony is that those who had been scattered preached the word wherever they went." This same group, which had been scattered, took the word with them.

Sometimes, readers, the press will get worse the more we resist. Sometimes, the stronger we become and the better we try to be, the harder the enemy will try. And, this just comes with the territory. We have to remember that we were sought out by God for this lesson, and we must emerge with our sense of self in tact. Only then can we apply what we've learned to a stronger, more effective persona, which is what God intends us to do. Only then, can we take this strength forward into the world and into the lives of others, furthering ourselves and furthering God's message.

READER'S PAUSE

LIVING WELL: EMBRACING ADVERSITY AND GROWING STRONGER FOR IT

Talk about adversity, in general, here. What do you fear? What do you see as problems in your life?

____

____

____

What, if given the chance, would you have done differently in the past when faced with a difficult situation? Tell us about your past issue(s) here and be honest about your analysis regarding what you would have done differently.

____

____

____

____

What we need to note is that the people of God did not allow adversity to strip them of their identity. While they were in Jerusalem, they were the church. They were the church, because on the day of Pentecost, the Spirit fell on them. This gathered church met daily together. They ate together. They shared their resources. They even sold their possessions collected the proceeds and created the first benevolent fund. This was the church gathered. They went from house to house. They continued, steadfastly, in the apostle's doctrine. They fellowshipped. They maintained their identity in the comforts of Jerusalem.

Suddenly, however, they were the church scattered. Would the church still be the same scattered like they had once gathered? It's easy to be the church gathered. Gathered, we pray together. Gathered, we have each other. Gathered, we sit in the comforts of these four walls. But... the church can't be gathered forever. There comes a time when we do have to scatter. Do we maintain our identity when we are scattered? Do you maintain your identity Friday nights at the club? Do you maintain your identity on vacation on the tropical Island? Do I maintain my identity at work when the pressure is on? Do you maintain your identity at home when the family is getting on your nerves? In worship, I affirmed the fact that I am a child of God in front of everybody, but do I affirm that when no one is looking? Can I hold on to who I am when there is no external pressure to be who I am? Of course I do. Of course we all do. It is how we keep the church with us, gathered, if you will, within us; it is how we reach out with what we do in worship and in faith.

AND WHAT, EXACTLY, DID ADVERSITY DO FOR EVERYONE?

In the bible, we need to see that adversity did not make them forget who they were. They were the people of God in trouble or not in trouble. It would have been tempting for them to become discouraged about their issues. They had to leave their homes. They had to uproot their families. Families were split up. It would have been tempting for them to give up on this "Jesus thing". But, they maintained their identity in adversity. Even when things don't work out the way you had planned them, you have to know how to maintain your identity. You are a child of God even in the trouble. Sometimes we lose it in the midst of trials—even the best of us do. It's how we pick up the pieces that matter.

They were scattered, and they took the message of the gospel with them. They kept doing in adversity what they had been doing in prosperity. In the relative comfort of Jerusalem, they were talking about Jesus, now having been scattered, they were doing the same thing. Can you pray in adversity the way you did in relative comfort? Lifting up holy hands is not just for days of being well; it's for sick days too! Can you keep coming to church in trouble like you did when things were all right? Praise is all weather! Shouting is all weather. It's for any season. They kept being who they had been; they kept doing what they had been doing. We can do that too. We can pray when we are down, and we can keep coming to church in faith when times are bad. We can reach out to help others even when we have our own pain.

WE MUST MAINTAIN OUR TESTIMONY TO GOD EVEN WHEN WE FEEL THAT WE HAVE BEEN "SCATTERED" BY ADVERSITY AND PERSECUTION

The persecution "scattered them." This word "scattered" is the word most often used for the sowing of seed. It is the word used in the parable when the sower "sows", plants, or scatters seed. The seed has something in it that makes it reproduce what it is. When the people of God were scattered, they couldn't help but doing what they did, because they had something in them that needed to be spread—that would thrive when scattered. They were going to reproduce and be fruitful no matter what, because when the enemy scattered them, they were scattered as seed—fruitful, nourished with faith, and ready to grow new ideas wherever they were sent. What was in them was going to come out. Locked in them was the reproductive material of the kingdom. Wherever you planted them, they were going to produce something. That's the nature of the child of God. Because of who we are and what we believe—what we have learned and what we can teach—we can produce no matter where we are planted. Some of us have been planted in some undesirable strange places, but from there, we were productive. We took adversity and made it work for us. We've done it before and can do it again. How many times have we been knocked down by problems or left to feel scattered and on our own in times of need, and we did well—prospered even—thrived in the face of adversity? English writer and preacher, John Bunyan, was "scattered" to Bedford jail in England. But, from that jail came the book "The Pilgrim's Progress", which is second in circulation only to the Bible itself. He overcame persecution and incarceration to live and thrive in order to spread his word and the Word of God. Like him, we are seed, so no matter where we are placed, something is going to be produced. Some of us have been scattered to some odd places and placed in some terrible circumstances, but with God's backing and our deep faith in Him, we have been able to continue our lives and our testimony to Him.

Like us, these were the people of God who were scattered. They were fruitful, because they spread the Word. They believed that the church scattered should infiltrate the world with the gospel. Sparked by their enemies and moved to action by adversity, they moved the Word of God forward. Note here that these were not the official preachers who were spreading the Word. We know that the apostles were not scattered, because they stayed in Jerusalem. The ordinary folks—like all of you—were spreading the Word, not the ordained clergy. The church can't pay preachers to do what God has called the people to do. Every time we leave our places of worship, we are to infiltrate the world with the Word; we should feel called to do God's work in all aspects of our lives. We should go to work with it! We should go home with it! Wherever they went—so did the Word. We can do this too. We can overcome—we can grow stronger—and we can spread the Word. What goes with you wherever you go? When's the last time you shared the word with someone? What word do we share? It is the word that Christ died for our sins and was raised from the dead! What do you take with you wherever you go? Stop taking the gossip! Stop taking mess, and take the kerygma. Take the Gospel. In the midst of adversity, the church maintained its identity.

"On that day, a great persecution broke out; those who had been scattered preached the word…" Their trouble had an upside, because they maintained their identity. Their trouble also had an upside, because

God was sovereign in the midst of adversity. In the midst of this trouble, God was working. In Acts, chapter one, the disciples ask Jesus when the kingdom will be restored to Israel. Jesus says to them, "it's not for you to know when the kingdom will be restored, that's in the hands of the Father." He goes on to say, "but you shall receive power after that the Holy Spirit comes on you; and you will be my witnesses in Jerusalem, Judea, Samaria, and the uttermost parts of the earth."

The persecution forced the people to go to Judea and Samaria. While in Judea and Samaria, they became witnesses. The word had already been going around Jerusalem. The mandate to get the word to Jerusalem had been obeyed. Jerusalem was working well. But, now it was time for growth. Maybe the church would have become comfortable with life in Jerusalem. Maybe they would have settled for life in Jerusalem. But, now it was time for growth. Growth only occurred because of trouble. Struggle forces them to become something more than they could have imagined. Struggle forces us all to grow. Unfortunately, many times in life, we want to avoid struggling ourselves or we want to relieve our kids of a struggle, but that lack of struggle often results in little growth. The story of the man who was observing the cocoon learned this valuable lesson: There was a man who found a butterfly cocoon, and he watched it for several days. One day, he noticed that tiny opening appeared in the cocoon. For several hours, he watched the butterfly struggle to get out of the cocoon. It worked its way through the tiny hole, but then the progress stopped. To the man, it appeared as though the butterfly had gone as far as it could go, so he decided to help the butterfly. He got some scissors and cut what was left of the cocoon, and the butterfly emerged effortlessly. When the butterfly came out, the man noticed something strange: the butterfly's body seemed swollen, and the wings shriveled up. The man watched the butterfly, hoping it would fly. But it never happened. The butterfly spent the rest of its life crawling around with a swollen body and deformed wings. What this man, who thought he was helping the butterfly, did now know was that the struggle of the butterfly to get out of the constricting cocoon was God's way of forcing fluid out of the body into the wings which would strengthen it to fly. Without that struggle, there would have been no growth. IN helping the poor creature, he had actually doomed it to a life on the ground with no wings—no sense of independence. In truth, we don't like trouble—we don't like struggle—we don't like adversity—but struggle is what gives us our wings. Some of us are grounded, because we haven't been through anything, or we sought release pre-maturely. Struggle in Jerusalem is what moved the church to another level of growth. James was right "count it all joy when you fall into multi-colored trials. Knowing that the testing of your faith worketh patience…" Someone can fly today because of his or her struggles!

It was God's intention to get the church to Judea and Samaria, but it took persecution to get them there. Their destiny was Judea. God had already told them where they were headed. He told them where He was trying to get them. That actualization of their destiny, however, was going to occur through some very strange means. I'm sure that they were excited when they heard about where God was taking them, but they never knew what they were going to have to go through in order to get there. God works in some strange ways. We never know how God is going to get us to where he wants us to be. God is sovereign over life's experiences.

Which means He may use what we're going through in life to finally get us to our intended destinations. The only thing the disciples may have had in mind was getting to Judea, but they did not know that they had to get through all sorts of trouble in order to get to their intended final destination. We get excited about getting to somewhere, but we don't understand that we may have to go through some difficulties to get there. Too many of us give up when we go through anything, and we miss out on where God is trying to get us to be. These people in the Bible who we look to for guidance, they had to go through persecution in order to get to Judea. None of us can faint while we are going through these difficulties; we can't fold while we are going through it all. We need to keep our minds on Judea and Samaria. The upside of trouble is that it may be the very thing, which catapults us into our intended destinies. Maybe the disappointment fits into God's plan for all of us. I'm not saying that for certain all the time. But, it is true that the journey toward the destination is not always pleasant. You can't miss out on the destination, because your journey is difficult.

I know the disappointment is heartbreaking, but God can use some ugly experiences to accomplish some beautiful purposes. I'm sure that the persecution in Jerusalem was viewed as a tremendous setback, but the longer the people then looked, the more they saw that the great purposes of God are accomplished in some mysterious ways. With setbacks, we have to stay vigilant and keep looking. When we keep looking, things that did not make sense begin to make sense. Job said, "I looked and saw that my family was gone, my finances were gone, my flesh was gone, and my future was gone. But I kept looking, and I learned some lessons

God was trying to teach me. I kept looking and what I lost was restored." You have to keep looking; you have to keep watching when you've been through. A setback may not be the negative experience we all think it is; it may be the gateway to something better. The upside of trouble is not immediately apparent. You have to give time to work it out! Give setbacks a chance! Embrace whatever you have been given by God to handle; you may be the better for it.

The enemy meant for the persecution to destroy God's work, but it actually served to expand God's work! What a mighty God we serve! God reverses the intent of the enemy. The enemy did not know that he was playing into God's hand. God can do it. Whatever the enemy intends for you, God can reverse it for his own purposes. There was an upside to the trouble. The Word got out. Philip connected with the Ethiopian. Joy was in the city. This was the upside to persecution.

The cross was bloody. The day was dark. Our Lord and Christ felt abandoned. The pain was unbearable. And the upside was not immediately apparent. There appeared to be no upside on Friday and Saturday. But, you have to keep looking. Something happened on Sunday. The upside of the cross was victory. The upside of the cross was a new cosmic equilibrium. The upside of the cross was the grand re-opening of our endemic paradise. The upside of the cross is new life. The upside of the cross is the defeat of death. What is the upside of the cross? Some of you have experienced the upside of your trouble. And now you have a testimony "through it all; through it all I've learned to trust in Jesus…" We must always trust in God's path for us.

9

WHAT ARE THEY SAYING ABOUT US!

In 1957 writer, educator, and philosopher, Bertrand Russell, published a book entitled "Why I Am Not A Christian." In this work, Russell delineates and describes the reasons he has issues with Christ, Christianity, and the Church. To back his argument for not being a Christian, he says everything from the fact that he believes that Jesus was no wiser than Buddha or Mohammed to the fact that the church is characterized by social irresponsibility and cowardly sexual ethics. His opinion is a strong one and maybe one that we or another we know has shared in the past—while either searching for God—going through a hard time—or just questioning new material when we join a new church or make a big change in life.

Russell's work reminds me of how it is not unusual for society to have a myriad of opinions about the church. Everybody from the old man sitting in the barbershop to the professor of philosophy at the local university has something to say about the church, and, many times, it is negative. The church has been the object of criticism for centuries. Marx said that the church and religion itself are nothing more than the opiate of the people. Lenin said the church is for grandmothers, and that the church would die with the grandmothers. Literary works from Chaucer's Canterbury Tales to James Baldwin's "Go Tell it On the Mountain" have implicitly and explicitly criticized the church. I must admit that some of the criticisms of the church are accurate and justified. The church, throughout the generations and even unto this present age, has brought some criticism on itself. Nevertheless, it is astonishing to me that so much has been said about the church throughout history. Does it make any of you think about our beliefs present day or in our own churches and congregations: I wonder what they say about us?

The church has been criticized as being too conservative in some cases and too liberal in others. The church has been called too passive in some generations and too radical in others. In some cases, the church's wealth is criticized. The clergy are criticized. Storefront churches are viewed as being too colloquial and narrow-minded. Mega churches are criticized for being too cultish and too concerned about money. The world always has an opinion about the church—no matter what form it takes.

The world always has an opinion about the church –no matter what form it takes.

Even when the naysayers are quiet about the church that, in itself, is an opinion. When society is saying nothing or when the community is silent concerning the church, this often means they are indifferent and feel as though the church is irrelevant. It is concerning when nothing is said about the church. It makes me and others wonder whether it means people aren't noticing change and movement in the church. In fact, one sure way for the church to stay out of the line of criticism is to just do nothing. When people or churches—organizations of any kind—fear criticism and attacks, they freeze. No one starts any new programs—they build any new buildings—and they don't speak out on any issues. And this is dangerous, because we run the risk of letting the world pass us by as though we and the church we believe in are some fossilized monuments to the past. Any church that is seeking to make a difference in society will be criticized. The world will try to find something wrong with it. Nothing will be said, however, if we aren't doing anything, saying anything, or being anything. So again, I wonder what they say about us, if anything? If we are being talked about (personally, in our churches, or in our communities), then we may just be doing something right.

OUR SCRIPTURE REFERENCE

In turning to the Bible for guidance, we can examine the church, in Acts 17:5-9 (NRSV), as it is embodied in its leaders and masses of people, was on the move and consequently became the target of criticism. The church had been moving from place to place and had some good experiences and some bad ones. In places like Pisidian Antioch, ministry did not go so well. Some of the citizens of that region had issues with the church's doctrine and practice and consequently expelled everyone in the church out of their town. These missionary preachers knew what to do. They didn't cry about it. They did not become bitter when things did not work out the way they had anticipated. They shook the dust from their feet and moved on to the next opportunity. They would not allow anything negative from the previous experience to cling to their psyches, so they shook it off. But, it's not always easy to shake off, is it? Even when we know that doing good work may invite criticism.

In places like Philippi, ministry went well. God moved, lives were changed, and churches were established. In Philippi, they had impact on the lives of Lydia, the slave girl who was possessed, fellow inmates in the Philippian jail, and the jailer himself. But, even though they experienced success in Philippi, when it was time to move on, they moved on. The last line in chapter 16 reads, "...then they left..." They could not rest on what had happened in that particular location. They couldn't keep celebrating; they couldn't keep having anniversary commemorations of the Philippian victory. They had to move on. A church can't keep talking about what it did forty years ago. The question is "what have we done for Him lately?" The truth of the matter is that ministry knows of both seasons of disappointment and seasons of great success, but in either season, you have to keep it moving.

We should note that Paul and his partners were strategic in their missionary work. They would pass through places like Amphipolis and Apollonia and make it to a place like Thessalonica. Paul wanted to get to some of the key cities, believing that if the Gospel could take root in these cities, it would spread to some of the smaller surrounding towns and outposts. So, when we do examine this passage, we find Paul and Silas in Thessalonica. It is in this city where we discover what the world is saying about them and what they ought to be saying about us! The criticism labeled against them is one we want hurled at us! They are spreading the Word of God, despite great scrutiny, criticism, and even disgust.

In examining this text, we see that it all gets started because of a GATHERING CROWD. "But the Jews became jealous…." We need to note, here, that this is not all the Jews. Some of the Jews believed in this city. This passage refers to the Jews who did not believe. As was their habit, Paul and Silas went into the synagogue to preach on the Sabbath. Paul was partnered with Silas instead of Barnabas, as we know from scripture. He and Barnabas had a conflict, and they were no longer working together. Even in fruitful churches. There can be interpersonal conflicts and misunderstandings between those who are supposed to be working together. And this, too, is fine. Again, believing something so vehemently will often cause arguments or differences of opinion. As long as they stay positive and focused in the same general direction, they are not serious. As we all know, when they become so big that one group is harshly targeting another, then it is serious.

So—in the synagogue, Paul reasons with the hearers: That is to say he asks and answers questions. Paul also explains the scriptures by opening them up for discussion and, yes, scrutiny. In doing this, Paul proves the Word to them by laying down evidence, and then, he finally announces the Gospel. Whatever he did in this passage—at this time—in this precarious situation, it worked for some of the Jews and the God-fearing Greeks, and the influential sisters believed and embraced the Gospel. It was a successful revival. Again, we don't always enjoy this type of inclusion and acceptance, but attempting to spread the Word is what we must always focus on—no matter what we feel people are saying or feeling about us.

Attempting to spread the Word is what we must always focus on–no matter what we feel people are saying or feeling about us.

However, once again, not everyone was happy with this success. Remember: "But the Jews became jealous...." They were jealous, because these people who had become believers were suddenly leaving the synagogue. These people who had been tithe-paying parishioners at the local synagogue were leaving! The primary issue with Paul's opponents was not doctrinal. However, it was personal. These folks were intimidated by Paul's success. These were Jewish preachers who were upset that folks were leaving their place of worship and going after Paul and this new Gospel.

SUCCESS AND INTIMIDATION

Some people are intimidated by success. It's sad, but we do often think that—as long as I'm not successful, folks will get along with me—no one will give me a problem. We often feel that we lose friends the moment we start doing well—or feel that we are being unfairly judged for doing well. Sometimes, it appears that people can only relate to others as long as they feel they are better than or on the same level as their peers. I suppose change is always a bit tricky, but if the moment you start moving ahead, and people start calling you "stuck-up" or going further and finding things wrong with you, it might be time to re-evaluate relationships—just like we learned in our biblical text in this chapter. If some people can only be your friend as long as you are struggling—broke—enduring substance abuse—dealing with a recent job loss or family trouble—then it is time to move away from that negativity. Certainly, you don't turn your back on people, but if you have a role in life as—a father, mother, teacher, counselor, friend, you can't entirely turn your back on others, but you can't focus on those who are negative either. Your message has to move forward just as we were taught in the biblical text we're examining in this chapter. It is OK to shine a bit without criticism. People on both ends of this conflict need to, ultimately, realize that.

READER'S PAUSE

LIVING WELL: HOW TO ACHIEVE SUCCESS

List below the steps you can take to make yourself more successful in the future. Make your first list a one-year plan—your second list a five-year plan—and your final list a ten-year plan.

One Year:

WHAT ARE THEY SAYING ABOUT US!

Five Years:

Ten Years:

In re-examining our text, we can acknowledge that some of those of the Jewish faith in this story, normally in control of their synagogue and their people's beliefs, were jealous. They couldn't handle the success of Paul and Silas nor could they understand what they were preaching. And while it is definitely OK to question others or not believe in what another does, your level of maturity is measured by your ability to celebrate another's success. In this case, Paul and Silas were experiencing success in an area where these of the Jewish faith wanted to be successful. And, this is difficult. When anyone wants so badly to be successful in an area in which someone else is excelling, it can be painful. For example, it is much easier for me to celebrate the success of NBA great, LeBron James, than it is to celebrate the pastor down the street who is having better success in ministry. That doesn't mean, however, that I shouldn't celebrate that other minister's success –maybe even learn from him. LeBron James' success is not in the area where I want to be successful. I'm not looking to play in the NBA. I can celebrate his success, but can I celebrate the brother or sister who is booming in ministry in a way that I'd like to be booming? It takes maturity to not be intimidated by someone who has what you want or is doing what you want to do.

It takes maturity to not be intimidated by someone who has what you want or is doing what you want to do.

Some of these of the Jewish faith are jealous, and they want to get rid of Paul and Silas. Therefore, they obtain the help of some "ruffians" or "troublemakers." These were folks who were just hanging out in the "agora", that is the marketplace, doing absolutely nothing. These people were enlisted for help in order to assist these Jewish religious leaders in starting a riot—when, normally, no one would approach these questionable people. And herein is another valuable lesson: When you want to start something—upset things—go to folks who aren't doing anything because, normally, they are waiting for some trouble. People who are busy and productive don't have time for trouble. For example, I was at a Knicks game recently, and during the game, there was an altercation in the stands. I looked down and noticed that the players on the court were still playing the game. Star player, Carmelo Anthony, was doing his job in supporting and playing for his team. However, the players on the bench had turned their heads in the direction of the fight in the stands. I noted at the time, and I'll relay it to you now: Benchwarmers have time for trouble but not those who are on the court! And this holds true in all aspects of life, doesn't it?

So, this mob of folks started an uproar in the city. What they did not realize at the time was that their way of solving the problem was creating a bigger problem—much bigger than the problem they were trying to resolve. Sometimes, how we handle a problem at home, at church, or on the job creates a bigger problem than the problem itself. You have to be careful how you are speaking when trying to deal with an issue. You have to be careful what you say when correcting someone or offering input into a given situation. You may do more damage than good, and this is what happened in this biblical event.

As we read, we see that this gathered crowd ends up lodging an IRONIC COMPLAINT. This mob goes looking for Paul and Silas. It is their intention to do them harm. They search all around town. Someone tells them that they believe Paul and Silas had been staying at someone named Jason's house. It is believed that Jason was one of the brothers who was converted through Paul and Silas' ministry, and that he was serving the ones who declared the Word to them out of his own appreciation. They search Jason's house to no avail. The enemy was looking for Paul and Silas, but they could not be found. They were still in the city. We know that because, later, it says that the believers sent Paul and Silas off to Berea that night. While the enemy was looking to do them harm, they were hidden. God knows how to cover you from the intent of the enemy. The enemy looks but can't find you and is left wondering why. God covers us. God hides us. God takes care of us. Sometimes you don't need more strength; you don't need more joy; you just need a hiding place. No wonder the Psalmist said "for in the time of trouble, he shall hide me in his pavilion: in the secret of his tabernacle shall he hide me; he shall set me up upon a rock. And now shall my head be lifted up above my enemies round about me…" The enemy couldn't find them. I wonder how many times the enemy has been looking for you and for me, but couldn't find us. God has his own "witness protection program" that looks out for His children.

God has his own "witness protection program" that looks out for His children.

In going back to the text, they couldn't find Paul and Silas, but they did find Jason. They drag Jason out and bring him and some other believers before the city council. They accuse Jason of hiding and harboring "those people who have turned the world upside down" and have come to their city. These folks did not mind the Christians doing what they were doing in Antioch. They did not mind them doing what they did in Philippi, but ... suddenly, they have brought this trouble to their city.

In the text, the criticism lodged against the Christians was that they had turned the world upside down. This is what the world thought at one time about this early church. To put it in perspective, this is what was on the front page of the Daily News. This is what was tweeted through the Social Media. This is what was being said at the hair salon and at the barbershop. This was BIG! "These are they who have turned the world upside down..." They meant it to be a criticism. But in the words of the late Caesar Clark, sometimes a criticism can be a compliment. I imagine that if Paul had been there and heard them say this, he would have said "thank you." They said of Jesus: He eats and welcomes sinners. They meant it to be criticism, but it was actually a compliment, for He did say, "I've come to seek and save that which was lost."

So, it wouldn't be a bad thing to say, "These are they who have turned the world upside down!" This is the best compliment that could be paid to a church. Of course, it is meant to be derogatory, but it becomes the highest of compliments. These folks were feeling uncomfortable, because the Gospel had stripped them of their securities. The Gospel, preached at it's best, makes you feel not at home with who you are. It makes you feel not at home with your sin. It makes you feel not at home with your dysfunction. It makes you feel not at home with your attitudes. It makes me feel not at home with my meanness. It is meant to do that—to encourage introspection and change.

Truly, in my experience, if preaching always makes me feel at home with who I am, then that is not the Gospel. If preaching always affirms me, then it is not the Gospel. If preaching always tells me I'm ok just the way I am, then that is not the Gospel of Jesus Christ. The Gospel of Christ evicts me from the house of comfort in which I've been living. The blessing is that it does not leave me homeless! It strips me of where I've been living, but it provides another dwelling place. That place is in the hands of the Lord! But, first and foremost it makes me feel like my world has been turned upside down. The Gospel turns everything upside down. If we've been standing on our own righteousness, the Gospel turns that upside down. If you've been depending on your own success to make you right with God, the Gospel turns that upside down. These Jews are accusing the church of having made the world feel uncomfortable with itself! What a great compliment!

About this church, the world says, "These are they who have turned the world upside down…" What are they saying about us? And then these accusers continue by saying how they've done it. This gathering crowd lodges this ironic complaint, and it is based on the fact that this church did nothing but PROCLAIMED CHRIST. They say, "these folks are acting contrary to the decrees of the Emperor by declaring that there is another king, whose name is Jesus." They say that the church is turning the world upside down by going against the grain. "They are going contrary to the decrees of Caesar…" This movement called "the way" is swimming upstream. They were turning the world upside down by being the alternative to the norm of society. According to the accusation, these Christians are a challenge to Caesar. It's difficult for the church to turn the world upside down when it is too close to Caesar. The implication is that the empire ought to be nervous when Christians are on the loose! Empires, that is institutions and systems of power, should be nervous when Christians are on the loose. School systems that have lower expectations of children of color should be nervous when Christians are on the loose. Governments that don't care for it's poor should be nervous when Christians are on the loose. Christians who are on the loose pose a threat to business as usual and that is a very good thing—a catalyst for change and forward movement—no matter what the naysayers do.

IN OUR SCRIPTURE, WHAT IS REALLY THE "HEART OF THE MATTER"?

And then these are accusers who get to the heart of the matter. Paul, Silas, and the rest of the church are not a threat, because they've been staging protests. They have not conspired in some military coup. They've only done one thing: they've simply been preaching Jesus as Savior, Lord, and King. How non-threatening that seems! On one hand, it is non-threatening, on the other hand, that truth does turn the world upside down. The accusers say, "They've been preaching another king..." "Another king" means one of a different king. He's not like Caesar. "He conquers with ambassadors, not with armies; His weapons are truth and love. He brings people peace by upsetting peace. He conquers through His cross where He died for a world of lost sinners. Caesar annihilates his enemies; Jesus died for His. He's a King who washed feet. He's a King who did not come to be served but to serve. As we all know, this King was born in the manger. He was royalty, but He wasn't born to royalty. When Prince William of England and his new wife, Kate Middleton, announced they were expecting a baby in 2012, there was a lot of hype. Kate's "morning sickness" made news. Speculation on the baby's hair color made news. The baby's name made news. All of this hype exists because the baby was born for the throne and is born of royal parents. Jesus is another King, though, isn't He? He was not born with all the hype. There was no doubt about what His name would be for the Angel relieved the parents of that duty by telling them that His name would be Jesus. He had hair like lamb's wool. There was no speculation and hype—just a humble King born to save us all.

So, again, the Christians are accused of turning the world upside down, but actually the ministry of the people of God was turning the world "right side up"! Actually, the world had been upside down ever since the story of Adam and his mistakes. The world was right side up before the fall of Original Sin, but now the world is upside down. Amoral behaviors—kids being gunned down in school—politicians playing partisan games with people's money. The Gospel has the power to turn the world right side up! A baby was born in a manger in order to turn the world right side up! We need to remember this, despite what they might be saying about us. We need to keep to our task as Christians and remember that it is the success and our ability to turn the world upside down that starts the buzz.

CASE STUDY 3

I'd like to tell a few stories—about change that moves us forward—and adversity that makes us stronger—and, above all, spreading the good word of our faith even when it is hard to do so.

Briefly, I'd like to touch on some of the adversity I see in my ministry and the change that often occurs as a result. I see mothers who have lost sons, children with no parents, or teenagers with nowhere to go at the end of the school day. I could cry with these people when they come to me in grief—wondering what to do next—or ready to give up, but... what I most like to assist with and what I most like to see is positive change—lives reordered and made right.

To the woman who lost a son, I often ask that something be done in his memory. Many times, all that the mother can afford in terms of time and money is a pay it forward type attitude when she finds that giving back by donating to charity or asking about her son's former friends is healing and making a difference in her community or her peer group. Other times, I see ambitious folks ready to start a rally, create a charity—even write letters to congress about violence, poverty, cancer awareness, education—you name it—they do it. In this way, the teenagers with no family or no home have hope either in receiving the grace and love of others or participating in the movement—the change. People grieving loss and dealing with terrible circumstances often turn around. I start to see them at church again, and I see a new light in their eyes—a renewed existence—the desire to find a new job, find a new apartment—rekindle with lost relatives and more.

Those who stagnate can never hope to achieve such enlightenment nor can they ever hope to see positive change occur in a timely manner in their lives. That is why it is ever-important to spread this good word—the word of your peers or those in need—the word of your committed family and friends—the Word of God—no matter what others think, say, or do. I've seen the power of the Word in action, and I know it works miracles—individually, holistically—big and small—far and wide. We are all the Voice of God, and we are all, in part, responsible for our own change and positive forward movement.

10

A RITUAL FOR REJECTION: SHAKE OFF THE DUST

WHEN FAILURE LEADS TO SUCCESS

For decades and even centuries, many people have been enriched by the sublime sounds, scriptural content, and rhapsodizing movements of Handel's "Messiah." At Christmastime, each year, you hear variations of the original score everywhere you go, which brings joy and cheer on all levels. George Friedrich Handel, however, did not compose this masterpiece in the comfortable context of joy and good cheer. During Handel's younger days, he was very popular and his operas were enthusiastically received. But around age 56, Handel's glory seemed to have faded. Nothing he produced met with any musical acclaim. It was failure after failure. But, he kept writing. In spite of his determination, there was still one disappointment after another. Because he wasn't producing anything noteworthy, he wasn't making any money. Because he wasn't making any money, he couldn't pay his bills. Because he couldn't pay his bills, he was being threatened with being thrown into a London prison. Due to the stress of indebtedness, his health started failing. He couldn't sleep at night. He suffered from severe rheumatism. Through all of his pain, rejections, and disappointments, however, he kept writing. He didn't give up on the prospect of composition. In the midst of this gut-wrenching time, Handel locked himself in his study for twenty-one days and wrote this majestic oratorio called "The Messiah."

Like Handel, anyone who has lived any amount of time, or has attempted some challenging things in life, knows something about failure, disappointment, and rejection. If you don't, maybe you haven't tried anything new. Failure, disappointment, and rejection are woven into the very fabric of human existence. Perhaps you've searched for employment to no avail or had some back luck in the arena of relationships. Some things just have not worked out for you. Maybe you weren't the one who was picked for something important to you. Perhaps you've been looked over or passed over for a promotion, acceptance to a school, or for a local award. Maybe, at some point, you even tried to make a business work, but it didn't. Perhaps school did not work out for you. If any of this sounds familiar to you, then I'm certain you have first-hand knowledge of disappointment, rejection, and failure.

Failure, disappointment, and rejection are woven into the very fabric of human existence.

Rejection, disappointment, and failure are real. They stare some of us in the face and make recovery seem daunting. But, the key is knowing what to do in the face of rejection and disappointment. People respond to dashed dreams and hopes in different ways. Martin King, in his sermon

"Shattered Dreams", says that some people react to rejection and failure by distilling all of their frustrations into a core of bitterness and rejection. Some of us simply become cold-hearted and callous as a result of things not working out. At this point, meanness becomes the dominating characteristic. When this happens to us, we stop trusting everything and everyone as we live life with the insipid taste of hurt in our mouths.

Some folks react to rejection and disappointment by withdrawing completely within themselves and becoming absolute introverts. No one is permitted to enter into these protected worlds. Detachment becomes a survival mechanism in which many people safeguard themselves from future disappointment and failure. These people are neither dead nor alive; they just exist.

Detachment becomes a survival mechanism in which many people safeguard themselves from future disappointment and failure.

Another way we react to failure, which on the surface seems healthy but is just as crippling as the other two, is ascribe to the fatalistic philosophy that says everything that has happened to us was determined by fate and is inescapable. People with this attitude just resign to the fact that anything—from failure to success to everyday life is unavoidable and unchangeable—"it is what it is". These people believe that life is controlled by forces completely out of our control. The problem with this reaction is that these people, inevitably, start feeling helpless and lose a sense of ambition even to the point that they may stop dreaming.

OUR SCRIPTURE REFERENCE

When the church in Acts 13:49-14:1 faced disappointment and rejection, they did not become resentful, but they did become introverted, and they did not resign to feelings of helplessness. They, in the spirit of Handel, kept writing. The church in Acts was a fruitful church, because they knew, for the most part, how to respond to rejection and disappointment. They knew what to do when a ministry did not work out. They knew what to do when a building project did not work out in the time they had imagined. They knew what to do if there was some ministry objective that did not pan out. Things don't always go as planned in churches. Things don't always go as planned in life. You and I have to know how to respond when things don't go according to the plan. You have to know what to do when you run into rejection or apparent failure. You can't give up or crack up; you have to know what to do. This church knew what to do.

You can't give up or crack up;
you have to know what to do.

Peter had his day, and suddenly, it was Paul's day. No one is irreplaceable; everyone has "his "day, and this was Paul's day. The leaders of the early church gathered in Antioch to pray and fast. As they were praying, the Spirit spoke to them. Things happen when the people of God pray together! The church prayed together when Peter was in jail, and we saw that the Lord blessed with deliverance. When the church prays together, the Lord blesses with direction. When we pray together, God will bless us with either deliverance or direction, amongst other things. While they were praying, the Lord told the leaders to send Paul and Barnabas off to do missionary work. They laid hands on Paul and Barnabas and then sent them off. (The church lays hands on servants of God when it is time for them to move to another level in ministry.) Upon being sent off, Paul and Barnabas preach here and there, and finally they make it to a place called Pisidian Antioch. And, it is there where they show us what to do in the face of disappointment and apparent failure.

In Pisidian Antioch, they are confronted with UNFORTUNATE REJECTION. However, it didn't look like failure when they started. On one Sabbath day, Paul and Barnabas went into the synagogue and preached Jesus unto them. The story of Christ crucified and resurrected is what they preached. Their preaching was so effective that after church was over, some of the Jews and Gentiles followed them to their lodging place, begging them to keep preaching. What a blessing it is for people to want more even after the Word has been declared! What a blessing it is when people have an insatiable desire for more of the Word. These people are rewarded as we see in our scripture.

What a blessing it is when people have an insatiable desire for more of the Word.

On the following Sabbath, the two were back in the synagogue preaching the Word. The news had spread that there was going to be some preaching in church that Saturday. People came from everywhere. The city was shut down when Paul preached. They had to put chairs in the aisles. They used the overflow section. Of course, not everyone was happy about the attention these itinerant preachers were getting. There was a group of haters around who started causing trouble. They could not handle Paul and Barnabas getting the attention that they felt they deserved. They could not handle the positive momentum that this movement was experiencing, and these folks started complaining to the chief men and women of the city. It does not take much to ignite a firestorm of bad publicity. We know this from present day occurrences. For example, in recent news, it was quite unfortunate that United Nations Ambassador, Susan Rice, felt it necessary to withdraw herself from consideration to be the next Secretary of State. All it took was the opposition—in this case, the John McCain's and Lindsey Grahams of the world—to talk disparagingly about her, and a firestorm of bad publicity was created. All it takes is a few people talking negatively in the church for reputations to be tainted or for initiatives to be tarnished. The tongue incites all kinds of trouble! We cannot fall victim to this type of mass hysteria, as we also see in our scripture.

A few people started talking, and, as a result, Paul and Barnabas were expelled from the city. They didn't walk out; they were thrown out. They did not give up on this situation prematurely. They did not leave because of hard times. They did not leave because things got rough—even though they were expelled. When facing difficult circumstances, it is tempting to walk out, to give up, or to let go, but we must be sure that we are not giving up prematurely. Paul and Barnabas stayed with it as long as they could, but they were thrown out. And this we need to note for our own lives.

READER'S PAUSE

LIVING WELL: WHEN YOU DON'T GIVE UP

Tell a story from your childhood when you did not give up and enjoyed a great outcome. Then, tell a story from your life as an adult when you did the same.

WHEN A PROMISING SITUATION ENDS UP NOT GOING OUR WAY

It is disappointing that a promising situation changed. Verse 49 says, "The Word of the Lord spread through the whole region..." And then Verse 50 says, "but the Jews incited...they stirred up persecution...." It looked like it was going to be the spot for success, but it ended in apparent failure. The failure in Pisidian Antioch would not have been so bad if it didn't look so promising up front. Failure, disappointment, and rejection are all the more painful, because things looked so promising at one time. It wouldn't be so bad if things hadn't looked so promising. At one time, the warmth and sunshine of possibility shone on you, but now the harsh coldness of disappointment chills your soul. Have you ever been there? Did it look promising at one time? You had one interview; maybe two interviews. But, then rejection! The child seemed so full of potential and life at one point, but then one or two bad decisions has led to unrealized possibility.

On top of that, it was God who led them to this place. They must have imagined that if God lead them here, surely they would experience success. This was a mess God got them into. There are some messes we end up in just by obeying God! Just because the Spirit leads us into certain arenas, does not mean we will experience what appears to be success. The presence of the "anointing" does not always translate into "success." Paul and Barnabas ended up dealing with disappointment and rejection in a place, which looked so promising, and in a place where God had led them! This is the trial and error in life that we must embrace—the rejection and failure that becomes part of us and makes us stronger—

teaches us what not to do in the future as well as what to do. The core of the passage, however, is not in the unfortunate rejection they dealt with, but it is in their FAITHFUL REACTION. It 's not simply what happens to us, but it is my reaction, which determines my destiny! We can't always control the rejection, but we can control our reactions.

So, in revisiting the text, we see that they are expelled from the city, and they show some level of acknowledgment of the failure. Right after they are thrown out, however, they do something strange. They literally take their sandals off and shake the dust off their shoes. Evidently, Paul and Barnabas had heard the command of Jesus when He told His disciples that ministry would not go well everywhere. He told them that when they went to a place and they weren't received, to shake the dust of that place from their shoes. Paul and Barnabas were prepared for rejection, because they paid attention to what the Word says. There are some things I could handle better if I just paid attention to what the Word says. The Word prepared them for disappointment; the Word will prepare you for disappointment. The Word says, "In this world you will have trouble…" I am not surprised by trouble, because the Word has prepared me. However, that same verse says "but be of good cheer, for I have overcome the world…" The Word also prepares us by informing us that trouble does not have the last word. Paul and Barnabas were prepared for the possibility of rejection. Some of you have not "cracked up" in the face of rejection and hurt, because when you didn't even know it, you were being prepared for the possibility of disappointment. Some of us may want to praise God for what God invested in us before we knew we were going to need it! I'm sure when the disciples heard that warning, they wondered if it was even relevant. Time will teach all of us the relevancy of the Word.

SHAKING OFF THE DUST

This is a ritual of rejection, which owns up to the fact that things didn't work out here. For them to shake the dust off meant that they were being honest about how things worked out. It wasn't some lack of faith that led them to admit defeat. Faith is not dishonesty. Mature spirituality can admit when it didn't work. This, as aforementioned, does not mean you give up on something prematurely. However, it does not mean that there is nothing wrong with owning up to the fact that disappointment and rejection are real. You are bordering on mental instability when you can't own up to failure.

At the same time, while that shaking the dust meant owning up to what happened, it also meant disowning it. You can't disown certain things until you own up to them. By shaking the dust from their feet, Paul and Barnabas are disowning the experience. Shaking the dust means "I'm putting this experience behind me." It means to rise above the rejection. It teaches us to sever ourselves from the pain and embarrassment of not having been successful. This ritual can be a sign that shows that we refuse to be contaminated by what just happened, so we should shake even the dust from the town we were just in—if it didn't go the way it should have, because we don't want to bring any of that with us—ever. And in this metaphor, dust doesn't seem like a whole lot, but enough dust can change the appearance of something. A part of our Saturday morning chores when I was young, we had to dust the coffee tables and end tables in the house. It seemed like such a meaningless task, but, after we had done it, we saw how much better the tables shined. Dust can change the way we look, the way situations look, and then enough dust can cause dysfunction. People tease me because I still listen to CDs. Sometimes they skip—not because something is wrong with the CD player—but because the CD has dust on it. Dust alters appearance and can cause dysfunction. That's why Paul and Barnabas shake it off. We need to note this in our own lives—how much of a difference keeping the rejection and disappointment—the dust—on us can make in moving forward in life and with God.

Paul and Barnabas demonstrate a level of acknowledgment, but they also display some activity. They don't just shake the dust from their feet; Paul and Barnabas also go to another place called "Iconium…." This is a place about 50 miles away from their current location. They couldn't just stay where they were and keep shaking the dust from their feet. We can only do that for so long before we—before anyone—has to move on. The topic of conversation can only be about Antioch for so long. They can only cry the blues about Antioch for so long. There comes a point where all of us have to move to the next thing. We can't move unencumbered if we still have dust of Antioch on us. Shaking the dust enables us to move on to the next place, but we have to know how to get "unstuck." Failure will have us all feeling "stuck". Rejection in one place will have you feeling stuck. You have to know how to move on. You don't want the dust of Antioch to mess up the possibilities of Iconium. Antioch is where we were—Iconium is where we are headed. In fact, Iconium is the new place where God is taking us.

There comes a point where all of us have to move to the next thing.

THE DAMAGE OF EMOTIONAL HOARDING

Paul and Barnabas demonstrate a level of acknowledgment, they display activity, and they also refuse to allow the experience to define their attitude. "...The disciples were filled with joy and the Holy Spirit...." "The disciples are inclusive of Paul and Barnabas, who had experienced the rejection. There's a whole lot they could of have been filled with, but they were filled with joy. As they move on to the next place, they are not moving on with bitterness. All of us know that we can move on physically and yet be living in what happened ten years ago. There's a reality show about "Hoarders". These are folk who don't throw away anything. They keep everything in their dwelling places—and in a very unhealthy manner. They can't even get around from room to room, because they hoard things. It is possible to be an emotional hoarder. It is possible to just collect experiences in your psyche, all of which really should be tossed out. This does not mean that you don't seek to resolve certain feelings. There are some feelings you have to deal with, or you just can't throw away. However, there are some things that need to be discarded. We all know that—we just have to put it into practice.

The text says they were filled with joy and the Spirit. The only way they could be filled with joy at such a time is to be filled with the Spirit as well. Being filled with the Spirit results in being filled with joy. The Spirit feeds our spirits. The only way to be able to still have joy after rejection and disappointment is to be filled with the Spirit. (The only way to be filled with joy in the midst of the tragedy of young lives being taken is to be filled with the Spirit.) They were filled with joy, because they were filled with the Holy Ghost. The Spirit is a joy producer.

This faithful reaction to the unfortunate rejection leads to a FRUITFUL RESULT. When the Paul and Barnabas get to Iconium, they go into the Jewish synagogue. That amazes me. After what the Jews did to them in Antioch, I would have understood it if they simply went and preached to the Gentiles. They would have still been doing ministry—just without the hostility. And here is how we know they are not harboring resentment or bitterness. They did not allow issues with some Jews to become issues with all Jews. In life, we need to realize that just because we've had a negative experience in one area does not mean that we should give up on that area. One bad relationship does not mean we give up on the possibility of a meaningful relationship, for example. When you have been jilted, rejected, betrayed, disappointed in a certain area, you have to resist the temptation to become cynical about that area. Paul and Barnabas went back to the same kind of folks who caused them their heartache in the first place and ended up doing the same thing they had been doing.

In the text, let's take note of Luke's language: "…Paul and Barnabas went as usual…" "As usual…" They went and did the same thing in Iconium that they had done in Antioch. "As usual…" For us, we need to realize that we can't let disappointment throw us off—we need to go back and do "as usual…" In your life, you may have had some hard times, but you need to go do "as usual…" Don't turn your back on possibilities; go do "as usual...." If you've been looking for a job, keep looking. You've been filling out applications for school, and you keep being rejected. Go back and do as usual, keep filling them out. You've been praying, and nothing has happened; just do as usual—worship as usual—praise as usual.

In closing, we need to remember that Paul and Barnabas go and declare the Gospel so effectively that a number of the Jews and Gentiles believed. God blessed them in Iconium. What we take away from this scripture is that even when you've been rejected—even when you've been disappointed—you need to move on, because our God is a God of other possibilities. We all have to shake off the dust, because God has something else for us! What a mighty God we serve. Let other people give up! Don't you give up, because God has something in store for you if you believe and maintain your focus.

Don't you give up, because God has something in store for you if you believe and maintain your focus.

11

HOW TO GET OVER IT AND MAKE IT!

DOING OUR YEAR-END REVIEW

The culmination of one year and the commencement of another year often provides us with the opportunity to look back and to look ahead at the same time. At one time, at one moment in history we retrospectively look back at yesterday, and we wistfully peer into the future. One of the things that happens when we look back is that we begin to wonder (at least for some of us) how we made it through certain experiences or certain seasons. In the words of that old song, sung by Aretha Franklin, "my soul looks back and wonders how I got over." While you were going through that experience, you never thought you would make it out. There was no way you could have made it through that situation. It looked hopeless. You gave up a few times. You were in the grips of the "dark night of the soul." Some people may have known what you were going through, but many didn't. When you look back, you can't help but wonder how you made it over. You didn't have the resources to match what the circumstances demanded. There were plenty of nights when you wondered how you would get to the other side of what you were dealing with. The pain was so intense. The loneliness was so thick. The uncertainty was so pervasive, that looking back, you wonder how you got over, got through, or got by. Sometimes you wonder because there are some other people who had to deal with what you dealt with and didn't come out the way you did. There are some others who lost their sanity, their faith, their families, or maybe even their lives. But, somehow or another, here you are.

Not everyone has had these types of traumatic experiences "yet." I say "yet" because all you have to do is to keep living, and, due to difficult times, may end up having the same testimony "my soul looks back and wonders how I got over." Perhaps this message is not even relevant to you right now. Maybe you've never been there, but just keep living. You may want to put this message in the freezer, because you don't know what tomorrow is going to bring. And, some of us don't have to look back at the trouble and trauma we've been through; nor do we have to look ahead at trouble we may have to endure; we are in the midst of it right now, and you are wondering how you will get through. If that is you, just keep going, and you will rise with the same testimony, "my soul looks back and wonders…"

OUR SCRIPTURE REFERENCE

In Acts 27:27-44, Paul and the others on board this ship probably didn't feel like they were going to make it through this journey to Rome. Paul, the prisoner, was headed to Rome to stand before Caesar to plead his case of innocence. There were many others on board headed to Rome as well. All they were doing was trying to get from one place to another.

That's all! Nothing else! Just trying to get from one place to another. As they are traveling, they run into some winds, which are making their journey difficult. They had not anticipated running into these kinds of winds. Perhaps they weren't totally surprised by the storms and winds, because they knew that when you are traveling across the sea, there is a very good chance that you may run into something you could not have predicted. Storms and seas go together. It would be unrealistic to think that you wouldn't run into something every now and then. The contrary winds end up extending the time of the trip. It wasn't supposed to take as long as it did. They had one timetable, but life had another. Along the way, the passengers and the crew on the ship made some bad decisions, which further put them in harm's way. Paul had even warned them at one point not to go a certain direction, but they did it anyway. At one point, the direction in which they traveled looked like the way to go, but it ended up being disastrous.

A PARABLE FOR LIFE: WHY WE CANNOT SUCCUMB TO OUR FEARS

Is this not a living parable of life? Sometimes all you're trying to do is to get from one place to another, and you end up running into some storms you could have never predicted. On the other hand, you probably shouldn't have been surprised, because storms are woven into the fabric of human existence. Along the way, you've dealt with some things, which have delayed the fulfillment of your destiny. You thought by now you would have been there. You thought by now you would have been done with that season of your life. But, the contrary winds have averted your plans. And then, just like the folks on board this ship, you have made some bad decisions, which have caused some unnecessary pain and trauma. Have you ever made any decisions, which furthered your pain? Your uncertainty? The irony is that some of these decisions were made in an attempt to get out of trouble. But, things ended up worse than before.

Sometimes all you're trying to do is to get from one place to another, and you end up running into some storms you could have never predicted.

The passengers on board this ship had no idea that they were going to make it through this experience. But, they did. The last line in the last verse of this chapter reads, "In this way everyone reached land safely." The question is "in what way..." I believe that the way they made it is the way some of us made it through. And I further believe that the way they made it is the way some of us can make it through what we are going through or through what we will go through. How did they make it?

They made it, because they did not SUCCUMB TO THEIR FEARS. At one point during their journey, the suspense was building. It was the fourteenth night having been caught in a fierce storm. It was dark. It was midnight. The strong winds were forcing the ship toward the shore. The crew took soundings and the water was 120 feet deep. They did it again, and the water was 90 feet deep. The situation was becoming more dangerous. As they drifted toward the shore, the threat of running aground became more real. Some of the crew had become so afraid that they devised a plan to escape from the ship. They just wanted out of the situation. Fear made them want to give up on the ship. It looked like it was about to go down. Paul found out about their plan to escape, and he said to the guard who was in charge "unless these men stay with the ship, they will not be saved..."

Fear will have you giving up on the ship. For fourteen days, they had been struggling with this particular storm. They couldn't take it anymore. After dealing with some things for a while, it is tempting just to give up. You devise your own plan as to how to give in, because fear has taken over. Fear took over on the ship, and they were ready to call it quits. Fear will have you making rash decision. They were not thinking logically. The plan was to try to escape the storm by letting down the lifeboat and trying to make it to shore in that. That did not make sense, because if you couldn't make it in the storm in the large ship, how could you make it in a tiny lifeboat. Fear will make you stop thinking. And when you stop thinking you will make rash decisions.

Fear will have you giving up on the ship.

READER'S PAUSE

LIVING WELL: HOW WILL YOU "MAKE IT"?

Now, it's time for you to list all of your positive attributes and features. What will help you make it in the near and/or distant future? What might hold you back? And… how will you overcome any challenges?

The only reason some of us have made it to this point is because we didn't succumb to the fears. The only reason some us made it through what we thought we wouldn't make it through is because we were not dictated nor directed by our fears. Fear wanted us to give up on the ship. Sometimes, the only way to make it is to stay with the ship. We all have to stay with the project. We have to stay with the possibilities of the situation, even when you are tempted to give up. Fear told them to give up the ship, Paul's word said stay with it. The only thing, which combated their fear, was the Word. When fear is taking over, I have to rest in the Word. The Word says, "God has not given us the Spirit of fear; but love, power, and a sound mind." In the midst of fear the Word says, "The Lord is my light and my salvation. Whom shall I fear? The Lord is the strength of my life. Of whom shall I be afraid? When the wicked even my enemies came upon me to eat up my flesh...they stumbled and fell..." In the midst of fear the Word says, "They that trust in the Lord shall be as Mt. Zion which cannot be removed..." The only thing that can combat our fear is the Word.

HOW DID PAUL AND THE OTHERS MAKE IT THROUGH THE STORM?

I wonder how they made it over? They made it over because they CONSUMED SOME FOOD. In the midst of the storm, they had not been eating. Since this intense storm started, they had stopped taking care of themselves. They were so worried about what they were going through that they did not think about food. V. 33 say "just before dawn Paul urged them all to eat..." it was still dark. As a matter of fact, it was darkest right before the dawn. The storm was yet strong. The night was yet dark. Yet, Paul encouraged them to eat. Paul says, "You need this food to survive…." He tells them that they will make it through the storm. However, if they don't take care of themselves, they will not survive. In other words, it's not the storm, which will kill them; it's worrying about the storm and not taking care of themselves. Sometimes, worrying will destroy us even before whatever we are worrying about does.

Sometimes, worrying will destroy us even before whatever we are worrying about does.

Paul tells them to eat based on the truth that they will make it out. He encourages them to take care of themselves by faith. The truth is they will make it through. It may not look like it in the present. But they needed to know how to take care of themselves by faith. You have to know how to take care of yourself by faith. The present gives you no reason to take care of yourself. Based on where you are, it is tempting to give up on taking care of you. But, you have to know how to take care of you for where you are headed. Even when it makes no sense to eat, you have to eat by faith. Even when it makes no sense to sleep, you have to sleep by faith. You have to get yourself together by faith. You have to know how to exercise by faith.

Paul tells them to eat, because they will make it. And when they come out on the other side of the storm, they don't want to look like what they have been through. If you are going to survive, you might as well take care of yourself, so that you don't look like you have been through or what you are going through. Just because you have been through hell, doesn't mean you have to look like it. Some of us like to flaunt our burdens. You don't have to do that. I am not advising that you are not real about what you are going through. It's ok to be real. But, you don't have to unnecessarily display your adversity in order to get attention. There were some days that I had no idea what my mother was going through. It was not because she was fake. It was because even in the storm, she had an uncanny way of taking care of herself, so that she did not look like what she was going through.

Notice the picture. The storm is raging outside of the boat; Paul is kneeling before the food on the ship saying, "God is good, God is great. Let us thank him for our plates. By his hand, we must be fed give us Lord our daily bread." He is thanking God for the food while the storm is raging. He is praying while there is craziness all around him. The child of God can maintain a sense of calm even when there is craziness all around you. You can still take care of you in the midst of chaos! Some of us can look back and declare that we made it, because even in the midst of uncertainty and pain you never stopped taking care of you. You ate by faith. You went and got your hair done by faith. You prayed by faith.

WHY DO SOME OF US MAKE IT AND OTHERS SEEM TO HAVE TROUBLE?

In what way did they make it? In what way have some of us made it? They made it, because they were THE RECIPIENTS OF FAVOR. After the passengers had eaten the daylight came. The daylight enabled them to see a bay close to the shore. They made for the shore. As they are heading toward the shore, the ship runs into a reef under the water. The bow was stuck in the reef, and the stern began to be battered by the relentless wave. They were close to the shore but couldn't make it.

The daylight had provided a little bit of hope for them. But, the hope is soon dashed by the battering of the ship. It's a bad thing to be teased by hope. It's discouraging when hope provided you with a little energy only to be drowned in the sea of further negative reality. Even with the rising of the sun, things got worse before they got better. They were stuck in this reef or sandbar right off the shore. They could see their deliverance but couldn't get to it. You can see it, but you can't get to it. There was a short distance between their destruction and their deliverance.

The ship was now being broken to pieces. What they had been depending on was now falling apart. It was one thing for them to be tossed around in the ship. That was daunting, but at least they did have the security of the ship. But, now what they had been depending on was falling apart. Have you ever been there? Have you ever just had to sit back and watch something fall apart which you had been depending on? Have you ever witnessed the destruction of the source of your security and felt as though you could do nothing about it? The ship was being destroyed and they could do nothing about it.

About that time, the soldiers planned to kill the prisoners on board so that they wouldn't escape. But a Roman Centurion, who really wanted to save Paul's life, prevented them from carrying out their plan. The passengers on board ended up making it because of some favor shown toward Paul. God's favor ended up blessing everyone on board because of the presence of Paul. The passengers on board are not even conscious of the fact that God's favor has saved them. They don't know that if it had not been for the favor of God, they would have never made it. God's favor is not always conspicuous, but it is powerful. You don't even know when you've been the recipient of God's unmerited leaning in your direction. Just recognize that you have been! God has leaned in our direction when we didn't even know it. God's favor has given many of us another year. God's favor has given someone another day. God's favor has blessed someone with another job.

God has leaned in our direction when we didn't even know it.

The experience of favor on the part of these passengers has nothing to do with them. It has to do with the presence of Paul on board. You want to make sure that you are sailing with the right people. You want to be sure you are hanging with the right brothers and sisters. You want to stay close to people who just look like God has favored them. Children, you want to stay close to some parents who appear to be favored by God. Joseph ended up being blessed as the legal father of Jesus, all because Mary was highly favored by God. And because Joseph was close to Mary, he ended up being blessed. Stay close to people upon whom God's hand seems to be resting. You may end up being saved because of whom you are hanging out with. You don't know how many times your life has been saved all because you were just around the right people. You don't know how many other people have been blessed around you, because of you.

Some of us can stand right now and declare that you made it because of God's favor. You can declare with confidence that if it had not been for the Lord on your side, the waters would have swallowed you up. It was not your money; it was favor. It was not your charm; it was favor. It was not your training it was favor!

My soul looks back and wonders, "How I got over." In what way did they make it? They also made it because they STRETCHED OUT ON FAITH. As the ship was being battered to pieces, the passengers were ordered to head for the shore. They were ordered to get there the best way they knew how. Some of them were to swim. Others were ordered to get on planks and surf their way to the shore. And still others were to get on "pieces of the ship". This phrase "pieces of the ship" is very intriguing. In the original language, it can mean literal "fragments of the ship." In other words, some of the people were to make it to safety just holding on to what had broken apart in their lives. Some of us have made it just by holding to what broke apart. However, figuratively, this phrase can mean "on some of those from the ship…" It is very possible that Luke, the one who is describing this scene, is saying that some of the passengers were to make it to shore by climbing on the backs of others who were stronger than they were.

If that is the translation we choose, the portrait of faith if remarkable. Some of the passengers had "swimming faith." Some of the passengers had plank faith. And some of the passengers only had climbing faith. But, all of them made it. There are some of us who have been able to swim to this point. Some of us did not have enough strength to swim, but you did have enough strength to ride on a plank. But, some of us had to depend on some other folks to help us make it. Don't get too arrogant, because you have been able to swim up to this point. The season may come when you will need somebody to help you make it to shore. And if you have enough strength to swim, you may have to help carry someone who can't make it.

And don't be discouraged, because you needed someone to help you to shore. God is so good that he provides help for you to make it to shore. Whatever the case, whether you could swim; whether you had to use a plank, or whether it took somebody to help you made it. You stretched on faith and made your way to safety. Somebody had to simply hold on to the broken pieces of whatever fell apart on you in order to make it. And those of you are still trying to make it, exercise whatever measure of faith you have. There are some days where you will be able to swim; there are some days where you may need a plank; and then there are other days when you will need to climb on a brother's back. But, do whatever you have to know in order to make it.

My soul looks back and wonders how I got over. In what way did they make it? They made it, because they did not succumb to fears. They made it, because they consumed some food. They made it, because they were the recipients of favor. They made it, because they stretched out on faith. Most importantly, they made it, because of GOD'S FAITHFULNESS. Before the storm, Paul told everyone on board that they would make it. He told them that the angel of the Lord told them they would make it. This was the word before the storm, and the storm did change the truth of that promise. Predicaments don't change the promise. Pain does not change the promise! Everyone making it to safety was not really about

Paul; it was not about the Roman Centurion; it was not about the safety of the ship. It was about the faithfulness of God. Would God be true to His Word? The fact that they made it was simply because God was being true to God. For anyone to have perished would have been for God to be untrue to God.

We've made it just because of God's faithfulness. Great is thy faithfulness; morning-by-morning new mercies I see; all I have needed thy hands hath provided. Great is thy faithfulness. And, readers, this we must take into the world with us. We know that we will enjoy better success by spreading God's Word and by listening all the time and accepting long periods of waiting or adversity in order to become the people he intends us to be. We don't always remember, however, that we can make it, and we have made it before. We have the tools, the fortitude, the experience, and the intelligence to handle all that God gives us, good and bad. Our faith sustains us and brings us to greater things.

We have the tools, the fortitude, the experience, and the intelligence to handle all that God gives us, good and bad.

CASE STUDY 4

WHEN THE WORLD FEELS LIKE TOO MUCH

I speak at a number of different conferences and engagements over the years, and at one, a woman approached me to talk about my discussion and presentation on trials and tribulations in life. She began her introductions to me by telling me that she felt blessed and was happy to be in the presence of so many people committed to praising God for their lives. She went on to tell me that she was a cancer survivor and had recently lost both of her parents. Her focus on this day was that her oldest child got into college and that her younger children were thriving. She felt grateful to be able to provide for them despite her single mother status. And she told me that the weekend, for her, was one of the most life-affirming and positive experiences she had been through recently.

We talked for a while. When she left to join friends, I watched her walk away—her frame slight, her gait strong and confident, her movements precise yet delicate—the picture of a woman put together and happy—yet... now I knew. I knew her secret—that her life was anything but easy—that she had every reason to be in tears or nervous and upset—that she had overcome so much in one year, it was a miracle she was still standing. At that moment, to me, she seemed vulnerable—so deserving of the relief she had in getting one child into college—or that her cancer was gone—that life was going to be OK even though she had lost both beloved parents.

I reflected on my own trials and tribulations on that day. For me, there weren't many. I had a lot of work to get through, my plane ride had not been great, and I hadn't slept well the night before, but… all in all, I was fine—I should have no complaints. And, yet, we do—all of us—every day. We do complain. Watching this slight woman with so much on her shoulders walk from me, happy, proud, and having a good day despite so many recent bad ones, really made me re-evaluate what was important in life—what we should worry about and what we shouldn't. My life, in comparison, was so easy. I took this feeling with me the rest of the day, and I do feel that it is a sentiment we all need to live with daily.

BIOGRAPHY

Rev. Jerry M. Carter, Jr. hails from Columbus, Ohio, and has served as the 14th pastor of the Calvary Baptist Church of Morristown, New Jersey since 1990. During his tenure there, numerous ministries have been initiated, and many lives have been changed and committed to Christ.

Rev. Carter's influence extends beyond Calvary. As a lecturer at the Hampton Ministers Conference, he has served as adjunct professor of preaching at Drew Theological School and an instructor of homiletics at Princeton Theological Seminary's Summer Institute. A number of preachers have attended his "How Shall They Hear" preaching conference, which is designed to impact preachers who impact churches that impact the world. Indirectly, he has inspired others through his published works in the New Interpreters Handbook of Preaching, Oxford Sermons Volume III, Evangelizing the Black Male in the 21st Century and the African American Pulpit. Locally, he serves on various community and clergy boards.

Rev. Carter received his Bachelor of Arts degree in Religious Studies from Denison University in Granville, Ohio, and completed the Master of Divinity degree at Princeton Theological Seminary in Princeton, New

Jersey. Continuing his education, he earned a Ph.D. in liturgical studies with special emphasis on homiletics from Drew University.

Rev. Carter is married to Melisa Rooks Carter, and they have been blessed with three children, Jerry M. III, Zachary Daniel, and Camille.